ISBN 978-1-332-30353-3
PIBN 10311508

This book is a reproduction of an important historical work. Forgotten Books uses
state-of-the-art technology to digitally reconstruct the work, preserving the original format
whilst repairing imperfections present in the aged copy. In rare cases, an imperfection in
the original, such as a blemish or missing page, may be replicated in our edition. We do,
however, repair the vast majority of imperfections successfully; any imperfections that
remain are intentionally left to preserve the state of such historical works.

1 MONTH OF
FREE
READING

at

www.ForgottenBooks.com

By purchasing this book you are eligible for one month membership to ForgottenBooks.com, giving you unlimited access to our entire collection of over 1,000,000 titles via our web site and mobile apps.

To claim your free month visit:

www.forgottenbooks.com/free311508

English
Français
Deutsche
Italiano
Español
Português

www.forgottenbooks.com

Mythology Photography **Fiction**
Fishing Christianity **Art** Cooking
Essays Buddhism Freemasonry
Medicine **Biology** Music **Ancient
Egypt** Evolution Carpentry Physics
Dance Geology **Mathematics** Fitness
Shakespeare **Folklore** Yoga Marketing
Confidence Immortality Biographies
Poetry **Psychology** Witchcraft
Electronics Chemistry History **Law**
Accounting **Philosophy** Anthropology
Alchemy Drama Quantum Mechanics
Atheism Sexual Health **Ancient History**
Entrepreneurship Languages Sport
Paleontology Needlework Islam
Metaphysics Investment Archaeology
Parenting Statistics Criminology
Motivational

THE LAND OF THE HILLS AND THE GLENS

BY THE SAME AUTHOR

THE
CHARM
OF THE
HILLS

New Edition, with
64 Full-page Illus-
trations direct from
Nature

A RAZORBILL GREETING THE MORNING SUN.

The Land of the Hills and the Glens

Wild Life in Iona and the Inner Hebrides

By

SETON GORDON, F.Z.S.

*With 57 Illustrations from Photographs
by the Author*

CASSELL AND COMPANY, LTD
London, New York, Toronto and Melbourne

First published *July* 1920
Reprinted December 1920

DEDICATED TO

MY GREATEST COMPANION
AND FRIEND

PREFACE

In the following pages I have attempted to portray some of the charm and the varying moods of the Hebridean coasts.

In the chapters the reader will find something about the wild life of that country, and I have also endeavoured to describe a little of the people and their traditions.

For the first two years of the war I was stationed on the Island of Mull, and in my duties of coast-watching there and on the surrounding islands had exceptional opportunities of seeing the country and of getting to know its inhabitants, for my work took me constantly to the most out-of-the-way places.

I can honestly say that I have never met with people possessing more charm and hospitality than those dwellers of the Inner Hebrides.

The Highland crofter or fisherman is almost always one of Nature's gentlemen, and is full of an altogether exceptional consideration and kindliness towards the stranger. In many of the coast-watchers I found firm and loyal friends, and consider that I was very fortunate in having such people to work with.

Since the war I have revisited the Hebridean Islands, studying and photographing the birds and renewing old friendships.

Certain of the chapters of the book, as "The Mail-Boat," "Ardnamurchan," "The Big Glen," "Skerryvore," and others, describe some of my experiences as Admiralty Patrol

Preface

Officer, though I have thought it better to avoid the mentioning of any matters in them which pertained to the war.

During the later years of the war, when stationed in Ireland, I had opportunities of comparing the dwellers on the western shores of that island with the West Highlander, and in the two Celtic types found much that is common. This was especially noticeable on and around the Aran Islands —a small group of islands lying west of Galway. It is here, too, that the two languages—or shall I say dialects?—Highland Gaelic and Irish Gaelic, most nearly approach one another.

There is an old saying that "the west's alive." Certain it is that the western seaboard and islands, both of Scotland and Ireland, have a charm that is ever present in the mind of him who knows them well, a charm which will always draw him back to the country known to Gaelic-speaking Highlanders as "Tir nam Beann, s'nan Gleann, s'nan Gaisgeach " ("The Land of the Hills and the Glens and the Heroes ").

Seton Gordon,
Late Lieutenant,
Royal Naval Volunteer Reserve.

Aboyne,
  June, 1920.

CONTENTS

Contents

LIST OF ILLUSTRATIONS

xi

List of Illustrations

THE LAND OF THE HILLS AND THE GLENS

CHAPTER I

SUNSET AND SUNRISE ON BEN NEVIS

AT one period Ben Muich Dhui was held to be the highest hill in these Islands, but with the advent of more scientific methods in the determining of altitude it was forced to yield pride of place to Ben Nevis, the summit of which, dominating the Atlantic seaboard of Scotland, stands just over four thousand four hundred feet above sea level. In reality, Ben Nevis has a great superiority in height over the first-mentioned hill, for at its base it is not more than one hundred feet above the waters of the Atlantic, whereas Ben Mulch Dhui rises from the high ground of Mar at an elevation of quite one thousand eight hundred feet.

It was early one afternoon in late July when I left Glen Nevis with the object of spending the night on the summit of the Ben. After a long spell of cold and misty conditions, an Atlantic anti-cyclone, which had for some time been struggling to dominate the weather of the Western Highlands, at length gained the upper hand over a series of small depressions, and a succession of magnificent days was the result. The walk up the lower slopes of Ben Nevis is comparatively uninteresting, though I noted that up to the one thousand five hundred feet level straggling birches clothed the hillside, and it was interesting to compare the limit of their growth here with that attained by them on **the**

The Land of the Hills and the Glens

Cairngorm Hills. As I gained the upper reaches of the hill the starry saxifrage (*Saxifraga stellaris*) and *Saxifraga hypnoides* were common, and an occasional plant of the parsley fern (*Allosurus crispus*) protruded its delicate foliage from between the rocks. For the last one thousand feet of the climb, however, vegetation was quite absent, hundreds of acres of volcanic "scree" covering the hill as far as the eye could reach. At an altitude of four thousand feet I watched for some time a number of ravens, apparently a brood of the year, accompanied by the parent birds. They were feeding on a spur of the hill, and as they rose gave an exhibition of soaring powers little inferior to those of the eagle himself.

It was near sunset as the summit cairn was reached. Even with the summer half gone, the winter's snow still covered the plateau, in places to a depth of quite four feet, and cornices of snow projected over the giant precipices. Though the sun had already set in the glens below, the plateau was still bathed in its soft rays, the snowfields in its glow taking on a faint pinkish tinge, Arctic in its effect. Lower and lower sank the sun in the north-western sky; passing just above the tops of the Coolin Hills in the Isle of Skye, and throwing out their peaks in strong relief, it ultimately sank behind the horizon across the hills of Knoidart at exactly four minutes to nine (G.M.T.). For a full three-quarters of an hour after this time its rays still shot high into the northern sky, and at no period of the night did the dull red after-glow disappear entirely from the horizon. A short time previously I had seen the light of the sun reflected on the waters of the far Atlantic, and now the hills on the Island of Rhum—the home of heavy stags—stood out sharply. Near by it was possible to make out a strip of the less mountainous Island of Eigg, and the hills of the Outer Hebrides, with their conical peaks—prominent among which was Hekla—were distinct on the horizon. To the east all was haze, save where a waning moon struggled, just above the horizon, to pierce the mist with her silvery rays.

By dawn the entire face of the landscape had changed. During the brief hours of darkness a pall of white mist, whose place of origin was the cold waters of the North Sea, had crept silently and rapidly over the hundreds of miles of country dominated by the hilltop. From this vast sea of mist the tops of the highest hills stood clear and sharp in the morning air. Such a sight as I was privileged to look down upon is one which is extremely rare in this country, and during extensive and varied wanderings on the Cairngorms at every season of the year, I had never once experienced like conditions, during which, more than at any other time, the lover of the grand and lofty in Nature has instilled into him the charm of the hills in its most inspiring form. Prior to the rising of the sun the mist was of a cold grey tinge. Then, gradually, almost imperceptibly, a rosy hue was imparted to the clouds beneath, and soon after sunrise the shadow of the Ben was projected on the mists for many miles to the south-west.

Scarcely a breath of wind stirred on the summit of the hill, but far below me the clouds were being guided westwards, and during their gentle progress assumed in places the forms of gigantic billows, rising above the average level as they slipped over some less prominent hill which barred their way. By ten o'clock the sea of cloud was as yet unbroken, and now reflected the rays of the sun with dazzling brilliance. High above the mist to the eastward the Cairngorm Hills were visible, Cairn Toul (4,241 feet) being specially prominent across the fifty miles of intervening country. Its contour was clearly seen— even the corrie of Clais an-t-sabhail, and, farther north, the slopes of Braeriach, with the large snowfield in the Horseman's Corrie. Across the valley of the Dee, Ben Muich Dhui was made out, the cairn on its summit being distinctly visible. To the south'ard of that hill Lochnagar held its top above the clouds, and just appearing above the summit of Ben Alder one could distinguish the outline of Beinn a' Ghlo or the "Mountain of the Mist," so named because its summit is often shrouded in cloud when the surrounding hills are clear. But the most prominent of the peaks projecting from the sea of mist was that of Schiehallion, whose tapering cone stood out with true Alpine effect. Westwards the twin tops of Cruachan were just visible above the clouds, but here the mist enveloped all but the extreme summits of the highest hills.

In the corrie of Allt a' Mhuilinn, far beneath one, the mist ebbed slowly backward and forward, seemingly endeavouring to press upwards to the higher ground, but making little, if any, headway. Sgor a' Mhaim, a few miles to the south-west, was prominent, its crater-shaped corrie being flooded in bright sunshine, and as I scanned this corrie through the glass a couple of stags were seen to gain the ridge and to look down into the white sea below.

An intense silence was everywhere; one missed the low croaking of the ptarmigan and the dark form of the eagle as he soared high above the plateau.

As compared with the summits of the Cairngorm Mountains, the absence of plant life on Ben Nevis is striking, for on the Cairngorms even the highest grounds are at this season tinged with red from the many plants of the cushion pink (*Silene acaulis*) in full blossom. Although the summit of Ben Nevis is quite devoid of vegetation, I came across a number of plants of the starry saxifrage at an elevation of quite four thousand three hundred feet, and a species of *Carex* was seen even above this height.

Among the precipitous rocks on the north-east face of the hillside a considerable amount of snow still remained, and, indeed, one of these snowfields has never been known to disappear entirely even during the hottest summer. The hill carrying the most extensive snowfields, as seen from my

EARLY MORNING MISTS FROM THE TOP OF BEN NEVIS.

THE MISTS ROLLI.\G UP THE GLEN OF ALLT
A' MHUILIN.\.

Taken from the Summit of Ben Nevis.

position, was undoubtedly Bidean nam Bian in the Glen Coe district, which, although not much over three thousand five hundred feet in height, must often, one imagines, retain the remnants of the winter snows in its north-facing corries throughout the summer.

It was to the east that the mist first showed signs of clearing, and soon rifts appeared in the sea of cloud, the green glens and hill lochs coming gradually into view. Of the sea lochs visible the Linnhe Loch was most prominent, and through the glass one could see the swift current flowing through the narrows connecting that loch with Loch Eil. Though a breeze had sprung up, the sky was unclouded, and as a result of the heat the edge of the field of snow near the Observatory had retreated a good six inches during the morning. On this field of snow a meadow pipit was for some time observed running actively around and picking minute insects from off the frozen surface of the snow, and about the same time a ring ouzel was noted to fly across the hilltop. Of the snow bunting I saw no trace, though doubtless he was not far off.

By afternoon the mists had gone, and hill and glen now stood out in the strong light; but the charm of the morning scene—when the world beneath was shut out in that silent mantle of cloud—had vanished, though in the memory it will be for ever retained as a rare and priceless gift of the Spirit of the High Hills.

CHAPTER II

THE EAGLES OF THE MOUNTAIN BIRCH

In a small glen, which lies, remote and secluded, in the keeping of the great hills, a pair of eagles have their home. Not during the whole year does the glen know them; it is only in the season of their nesting that they descend from the snow-filled corries and wind-swept plateaux that lie to the west of the glen.

Much time passes by during the nesting of the hill eagle. With smaller members of the bird tribe the eggs are laid, and the family become fully matured within the space of a month, but with the eagle the case is different. For six weeks she must needs cover her eggs before her young see the light of day, and even then, when the first part of her duties is over, her eaglets must be tended for more than two months before they are sufficiently strong to take their first flight from the eyrie.

Veteran, storm-scarred birches clothe the small glen. It is late indeed before these trees feel the impulse of life. When spring has already come to the plains, and the trees of the low country have put forth their leaves of filmy green, these birches still stand in their nakedness as they did in the first month of the year. In the oldest of these birches the eagles have their home.

On May 5 of a certain year I made my way through the glen. The hills held many a snow wreath in their corries, and the mountain loch was ruffled by a strong wind out of the south-west. The parent eagle was brooding on her great eyrie; so close, indeed, did she sit, that it was not until I was directly under the tree that she moved off, soaring out over the glen, and rising, as she circled, to a great

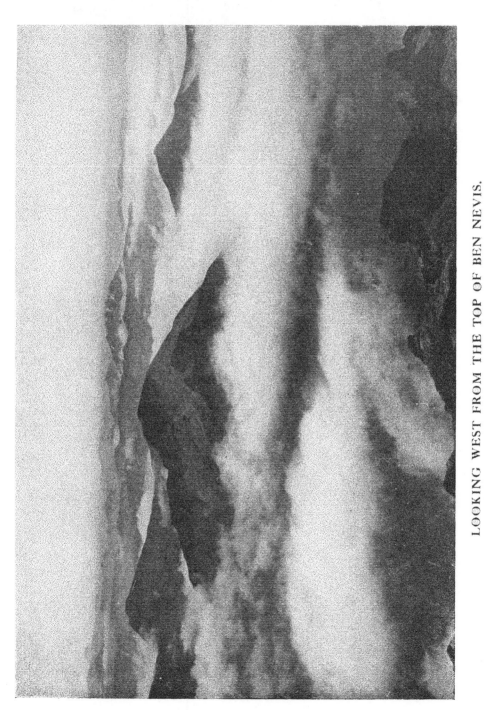

LOOKING WEST FROM THE TOP OF BEN NEVIS.

Sgor a' Mhaim in foreground and behind it Bidean nam Beann.

ON BEN NEVIS : THE SUN DISPELLING THE MIST FROM THE NEIGHBOURING TOPS.

height. Almost at once her mate joined her, and together they made their way to the snow-clad ground to the west.

There were two eggs in the nest—eggs remarkable for the beauty and clearness of their markings—and they reposed on a lining of fresh green pine branches and flowering shoots of the cranberry.

It was late in July when I revisited the glen. The birches were dark green, and many plants of *Saxifraga azoides* were opening their yellow petals. Across the hill a herd of stags moved anxiously, and a pair of kestrels soared gracefully near a rocky gorge where was their nesting site. Through the glass I could see one of the eaglets perched on a branch immediately above the eyrie. He was engaged in preening his feathers, unaware of the proximity of danger; but as I approached he showed uneasiness, and at length jumped down into the nest. For a time he watched me, his anxiety momentarily increasing, until the impulse to escape mastered feelings of caution, and he threw himself from the home that had sheltered him from the early days of May. A fresh breeze blowing down the glen troubled him somewhat, but he succeeded in reaching a point well up on the hill face opposite, where he made an ungraceful landing. Until now I was not aware that the eyrie contained a second bird; but as I reached the immediate vicinity of the tree the second eaglet began to crane her neck out of the nest, evidently debating whether she, too, could risk a voyage into space.* She was not so fully matured as the bird I first noticed, nor did her flight, when at length she left the eyrie, show the same power. She, too, crossed the burn and came to rest on some rocky ground on the far side.

I noticed a somewhat interesting fact as she sailed through the air below me—that her wings bore noticeably more pronounced markings of white than those of the first bird. An excited willow warbler flew restlessly among the branches

---

* *Note.*—When two eaglets are reared, I have always found one to be a cock and the other a hen bird.

of the birch tree, incessantly uttering its soft musical alarm note. It evidently was the possessor of a brood somewhere in the neighbourhood, and I wondered whether it was the same individual that had sung so energetically on the occasion when I was at the eyrie in the first days of May.

In the eagles' nest I found the fresh remains of a grouse, a couple of rabbits, and the feet of a mountain hare. A single branch of green heather, freshly pulled, had been carried there by one of the parent birds with the object of adorning the nest, which had certainly deteriorated from its fresh and clean condition, and gave off a variety of perfumes of a none too pleasant kind.

While I was at the eyrie the parent eagle moved restlessly across the hill-face opposite, and at last alighted on a raised piece of ground near the skyline, ruffling her feathers as she felt the full force of the strong and cool breeze, and peering anxiously around until, too restless to remain inactive, she again took wing and crossed the glen. I moved across to where the second eaglet was standing and almost stupidly surveying her new surroundings. A wheatear was expressing its strongest disapproval at the presence of the formidable intruder, and this disapproval was shared by a mountain blackbird and a diminutive wren, but the eaglet seemed quite unaware of the presence of those whose fury she had aroused, nor did she mark the rabbits of all sizes which scurried to their holes. As I approached, the young eagle walked up the hillside in a slanting direction, holding outspread one of her splendid wings in order the better to preserve her balance. I had ample opportunity of admiring the beauty of her plumage. On the neck the feathers, of a rich red-brown, were scarcely fully matured, and in her anger the eaglet repeatedly raised these feathers till they stood out sharply, showing the white of the down underlying them. The plumage of the back and wings was of a dark grey-brown, each wing showing two conspicuous patches of white, the central portions of the tail

Young Golden Eagle Defiant.

Feathers of the Head Raised in Anger.

ANOTHER STUDY.

GOLDEN EAGLE: "READY FOR THE WORST."

feathers being strongly marked with white also. The powerful legs were encased in snow-white stockings, with dark feathers covering the thighs. By manœuvring I succeeded in driving the eaglet towards her companion, and then approached the bird which had first left the eyrie. I was considerably surprised to see him sail out on a second flight as I neared him, and, as he was too strong on the wing to approach, I left him where he had alighted, and returned to his more helpless relation. I was anxious to observe whether this bird would be reluctant to cross the burn, and at length, by diplomacy, brought her to the edge of the stream. A sandpiper with a family near showed the most intense anxiety as we approached, fluttering up into the air and repeatedly uttering her shrill whistling note of distress.

For a short time the eaglet seemed to be suspicious of the murmuring water, but quite of her own accord she at length waded into and across the burn without hesitation. I left her there, with head almost touching the ground, in an attitude of grave thoughtfulness.

The sun had already gone from the little glen. Dark thunder-clouds rolled up from the big hill to the west. There was no sound now in the glen, save the rush of the burn and the cry of a ring ouzel, full of the responsibility of family cares.

For a time the eaglets are tended by their parents, but when they reach the fullness of their strength, and taste of the power of that incomparable flight of theirs, they are ruthlessly driven from the home of their youth by these same parents which formerly bestowed such care and affection upon them.

And with the coming of each spring the eagles will return to the small glen.

CHAPTER III

THE COMING OF SPRING TO THE MIST ISLANDS

Lonely and in the keeping of the great Atlantic is the island of which I write. During the wild gales of the winter season the spray from the swift-moving rollers reaches almost to the summit of the little hill—it is only three hundred feet high—which catches the low mist clouds that sweep in from the sou'-westward.

It was on a day of soft drifting showers, and that thick mist which brings the clouds so low that they seem even to touch the surface of the water, that I first visited the island.

For weeks, months even, during the season of winter the island is inaccessible, owing to the swell that breaks against its rock-girt sides even during fine, quiet days. But a spell of winds from the north had calmed the waters, so that it was possible to land this day of early January on the lee shore.

A curiously quiet and peaceful atmosphere brooded on this day of mists over the island. One seemed to be in the abode of the cloud-spirit, with only the boom of the surf and the sigh of the wind to break the great silence.

As I landed, a solitary oyster catcher flew out from the shore, uttering no cry. Above the hilltop there soared a buzzard and his mate. On the grassy plateau many barnacle geese stood, their feeding interrupted, and watched me inquiringly. Through the glass I could clearly make out their handsome plumage of black and white, with their bills of a black colour.

Soon they rose into the air, flying slowly and power-fully into the wind. Many cries were then borne across to

10

the ear; curious, sharp, though plaintive sounds, as the geese spread into line. Then, marshalled into order, they made their way towards the west for a time, but were unwilling to leave their island, and turned about, crossing over me at greatly increased speed, their many cries sounding as a confused, though musical, murmur. Backward and forward they flew for a while. At one time they were accompanied by a raven, the dark bird of wisdom moving with the flock only a short distance before he turned off and hung, looking for all the world like a peregrine, in the teeth of the wind.

Sometimes the mist curtain lifted somewhat, and then the hills of the mainland showed themselves.

Snow rarely visits the island, and even in January the grass was green and the great clumps of sea thrift were showing vigorous growth.

In the mild mist-laden wind one imagined there was borne the breath of the coming spring. The raven, at least, must have felt the impulse of life, for he, the very first of all birds to nest, must shortly repair his home on the precipitous cliff. Before February is out his mate will be brooding her speckled eggs, with the salt spray in her face and with the storms of wind and rain beating on her strong plumage.

But not for many months will the island throb with its great bird population. Every spring does the isle give itself over to countless feathered travellers, who leave the seas, where they have spent the winter months, and rear their young in its recesses. The puffin, after its long sea journey from beyond the Straits of Gibraltar, reaches the island during the first days of May, and almost at once sets about examining the burrow in which it reared its solitary child last summer. The black guillemot breeds on the rocks, and the storm petrel broods on its one white egg in the twilight that is present among the crevices of the great boulders.

The Land of the Hills and the Glens

The geese, too, remain on the island till after some of the bird people have already commenced family cares; and then rise calling, in a body, to make their way swiftly to the great uninhabited regions beyond the Arctic Circle.

It was on the second day since the coming of the New Year that the Spirit of Spring was unmistakably abroad, when I again crossed to the island group. Not a breath of wind stirred the waters of the Atlantic this February morning, and for almost the first time since summer no swell rolled shorewards. As I passed the ledge of rock where the raven has his nest, the cock sailed out over the face of the cliff, rising and falling on his powerful wings, and at times somersaulting in the air after the manner of a green plover. On the surface of the quiet waters black guillemots, many of them paired, were to be seen. Nearing the two small islands which lie most closely to the mainland, many barnacle geese again rose up from their feeding. Few birds that I know have a history as interesting as that of the barnacle geese. From very early times an extraordinary birth has been accredited to them—so extraordinary, indeed, that its origin must be, I think, a mystery. The belief prevalent was that this goose commenced its career, not as an egg, but as a barnacle. These barnacles, fixing themselves to floating planks in the ocean, were tossed around until, in due season, a minute gosling hung suspended head downward in the water. Although so minute, this embryo was fully possessed of the image of its race, and leaving its prison, rapidly gained the use of its wings and made its appearance as a true goose. So firmly has this belief been held that even to-day it exists, I believe, in some parts of Ireland. It is possible that the tradition may have had its origin in the fact that, until recently, the nesting site of the barnacle goose was wrapped in mystery—lying as it does in the inaccessible districts of the High North—

and it was probably because no eggs laid by the bird had ever been seen that the quaint superstition arose.

In the Gaelic the barnacle goose is known as "Cadhan," and a certain man from Mull, Callum by name, was wont to tell the story how that he swam for a week in the Indian Ocean (where the water is very warm) and that the most beautiful music he ever heard was that made by barnacle geese as they emerged from the barnacles which had attached themselves to Callum's feet during the swim!

As we passed slowly—the tide was contrary—through the maze of small islands, the sun shone clearly, and bird life responded to the warmth and quiet. Oyster catchers in their handsome plumage of black and white stood on the rocks enjoying a sun bath. On the summit of a cliff a buzzard stood motionless. Companies of turnstones flitted restlessly about. Above one of the islands I noted a snipe flying in such a characteristic manner that it seemed to me he must be "drumming," though we were too far distant to hear the sound. A pair of ravens appeared for a time, and grey-plumaged hoodies took wing at our approach.

On a small rocky island before us numbers of grey seals were lying on the flat rocks just above the water's surface. One after another they dragged themselves awkwardly to the water-side and dived quietly in. For the space of a little less than a minute they were hidden, then in quick succession heads were thrust up out of the water, and the boat closely scrutinized, though with little fear, by the seal population, some of whom, more inquiring than the rest, followed in the wake of the craft.

My aim this day was the most outlying and distant island of the group, and the sun was dipping to the sou'-westward before it was reached. Even in this region, noted for its storms, there was scarce a perceptible rise and fall of the water on the rock-girt shores. Indeed, the fishermen who were present gave it as their belief that rarely in their experience of the finest summer weather had they known the sea so calm here. But even to-day one could see, at a corner of the island, the water being driven at times through a narrow opening or "blow-hole" among the rocks, and being thrown out on to the quiet air in the form of finely-divided spray, which hung smoke-like for a while before returning to its parent ocean, and as we approached nearer the sharp sound of air and water forcibly expelled was audible. In the centre of the island a rounded hill rises a few hundred feet. On the summit of this hill a peregrine and his mate were standing, sentinel-like. One bird took wing, the other remained. Green cormorants, their crests raised, stood around on the rocks, and showed a remarkable absence of fear. One individual remained not thirty yards from where the landing was made, yet he did not take wing, nor even move from his position.

A faint breeze from the west was ruffling the waters of the Atlantic as the sail was hoisted for the return journey. Above circled greater black-backed gulls, uttering hoarse querulous cries. Then, after a time, we passed through the inner group of islands, sailing, in the failing light, between sunken rocks and through channels so narrow that only to a seaman with great knowledge of these waters could the helm be entrusted with safety. Two miles from land the night was still clear, the waters calm, and the lighthouse to our north a sure guide.

And then, without warning, a squall of sleet descended on us, coming straight from the high hills to the south. In less time than it takes to tell, every landmark was blotted out—even the strong glare of the lighthouse was hidden. Quickly the wind freshened, and with anxiety the fishermen spoke rapidly among themselves in the Gaelic. The jib was lowered, and we drove on through impenetrable gloom with increasing speed. Even the outlines of my companions in the boat were scarcely visible and one had a feeling of utter helplessness as the squall increased in strength and the small boat commenced to rock and creak in the rising seas. At length, after a very anxious time and to the great relief of all hands, a dim, hazy outline was discerned on the starboard bow, and with the passing of the squall we once more found our bearings, and, a little later, drew in the skiff to the narrow harbour among the dark rocks of the Atlantic seaboard.

CHAPTER IV

AT THE BREEDING GROUNDS OF THE GREY SEAL

STANDING out amongst the waters of the wide Atlantic there lies a small rocky island where, every autumn, the grey seals gather to rear their young. To many seamen the island must be a familiar object, for it lies fair in the track of an important trade route, and is a well-known and prominent object from afar. Lying near the island are dangerous sunken rocks, and not many years back it was proposed to erect a beacon there, but the idea has not materialized, and the rock is given over to the tribe of the grey seal. The seals are absent, or almost so, during the months of spring and summer, and it is not until September that they take up their quarters on the island's rocks.

In ushering its young into the world in late September, or during the early days of October, the grey seal is almost unique among the mammals of this hemisphere. Up to a few years ago its numbers were steadily decreasing, and it is probable that the seals would have been exterminated by this time were it not for the fact that an Act of Parliament, passed a few years back, makes it illegal to shoot the seals, young or old, from October 1 to November 30.

During the first week of November in the year of which I write, fine clear weather prevailed along the Atlantic seaboard—in marked distinction to the storms of wind and rain experienced on the East coast—and the waters of the ocean were untroubled by even the slightest swell.

Before the first light of dawn appeared in the east I started out on my way for the harbour, whence commences the long sail that lay between me and the seals' rock.

16

GREY SEAL, ABOUT TWO WEEKS OLD—TAKING REFUGE IN A STAGNANT POOL.

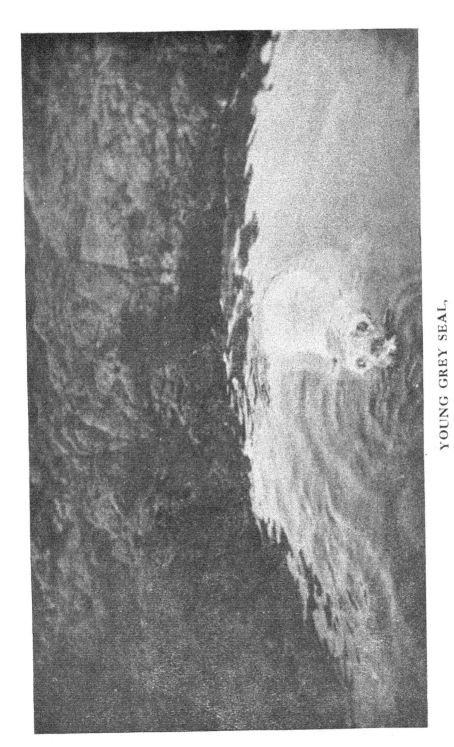

YOUNG GREY SEAL,

Completely Submerged in a Pool.

The Breeding Grounds of the Grey Seal

Gradually the light increased, showing up the distant islands bathed in a soft warm glow, until at length the sun rose from behind a great hill away to the east, and lit up masses of thunder-clouds lying near the western horizon. As we pushed out from the shore only a gentle breeze ruffled the sea, and it was not until the boat had rounded the headland that the sail replaced the oars. One remarked on the scarcity of bird life as compared with the summer months. No companies of puffins or guillemots flew restlessly past; no sea swallows hovered, flashing in the sunlight, as they scanned the clear waters beneath in their search for small fry.

An occasional shag flew heavily by, low on the water's surface, and we also passed solitary black guillemots, now in their winter plumage of black and white. In some of these the white colouring so predominated that from a distance they appeared almost like gulls. This seasonal change of the black guillemot is an interesting one, and it is difficult to see why the bird should assume a comparatively white plumage during the winter months, unless it be to harmonize with the white breakers and spume on the waters.

It was near mid-day before the breeding rock of the grey seals was reached. Numbers of greater black-backed gulls flew out on their broad wings as the boat neared the island, and a flock of barnacle geese, but recently arrived from their breeding grounds in the far north, rose from the grassy terraces and flew by us at a great height, calling softly and musically to each other.

It is seldom possible to land on the western side of the island, even in fine weather, for here the heave from the south-west travels right across from the American coast, with no land to break it; but on this day the swell was absent, and the boat could be pulled right in under the rocks. The breeding ground of the seal is a flat, rocky terrace, not many feet above high water mark, and on this terrace several young seals were lying, showing up very white in the clear sunlight.

The grey seal, when first born, is covered with a thick coat of cream-coloured hair, about one and a half inches long, but when the youngster has reached the age of a month or so this hair is cast and replaced by a shorter covering more or less similar to that seen on the adult seals. Approaching the youngsters cautiously, in the hope of having a view at close quarters of their parents, we surprised several of the latter, who hurried across the rocks at amazing speed, precipitating themselves into the sea before it was possible to cut off their retreat. One big seal had only just time to hurl herself into a pool, whence the only egress to the open was a narrow space between two rocks beneath the water's surface, and I stood above these rocks, attempting to keep her in the pool. The alarmed animal sank to the bottom, where she remained for some time motionless; then, without a moment's warning, she half rose to the surface, and forcing herself through the narrow and tortuous exit, swam like some great fish out to sea, throwing a deep ripple before her as she went.

Another seal was disturbed as she was suckling her well-grown offspring; she was some distance away from the sea, and her only refuge was a deep and stagnant pool, so full of green slime that the bottom was invisible. Into this she plunged and at once submerged. Minute after minute went by, and still she remained deep in the evil-smelling water, and it was not until quite seven minutes had elapsed that her head appeared and she gazed upon the intruders with large reproachful eyes, while she drew a succession of deep breaths before again withdrawing herself from view. It was interesting to observe that, after inhaling, the seal's nostrils could be entirely closed at will, this, of course, facilitating a long period of submersion.

Even before disturbing the colony it was noted through

the glass that several of the baby seals had their own particular pool of water, sometimes of small proportions and only a foot or two deep, in which they lay and wallowed. When approached and inspected, they dived and lay, not without effort on account of their buoyancy, with their heads a few inches below the surface, looking closely at us through the water with wide-open eyes. Their power of endurance was, naturally, much less than that of their parents, and after a short period they would emerge and quaintly attempt to scare one by blowing water through their nostrils. One or two individuals, the babies of the tribe, were unable to move from where they lay, with their cast hair scattered round them. They rolled over on their backs, staring angrily at us and uttering moaning cries. Sometimes a couple were lying in close proximity to each other, and in such cases it usually happened that one of the seals turned upon the other, imagining that its snarling was directed against itself.

It seems to be the case that the seal, when under water, rarely, if ever, closes its eyes, and this may account for the fact that in the majority of the youngsters examined the eyes were watery, and looked as though the owner was suffering from a cold in the head. The eyes of some were of great beauty, of a deep black colour. It was interesting to notice how widely the young grey seals varied in their colouring. In two individuals of the same age one was, perhaps, of a dappled grey, while the other was of a dappled dun.

No remains of fish were to be seen near any of the young seals, pointing to the fact that they are nourished entirely by their mothers for the first month or two of their existence.

One young seal, perhaps six weeks of age, was lying dozing in the sun near a pool of water. On being dis-turbed, he made determinedly for the pool, nor could he be induced to stop, offering fight to anyone who stood in his path and attempted to delay his progress.

During the time I and my companions were examining the young seals their parents showed great anxiety, constantly pushing their heads above the surface of the water and watching the intruders with their solemn eyes.

In size the grey seal is considerably larger than the common species. It is also relatively greater in circumference, its girth being almost equal to its length, while the brown seal is longer and thinner. In weight the females of the grey species vary from about twenty up to forty stone, while males of over sixty stone have been killed.

The young do not leave the rock for at least two months after their birth, but can stand prolonged exposure in the water. During the early days of November, 1911, and again in 1918, a severe westerly gale swept a number of young seals off the rock, and they were carried before the storm to the shores of the mainland. In some cases the mothers accompanied them, and presumably reared them safely after their trying experience.

The November day is short, and even with fine weather it is unwise to risk sailing in these exposed waters after darkness has set in, so my visit to the rock was of necessity a short one. Contrary winds delayed the homeward progress, and it was not until the sun had dipped behind the Atlantic and the rays of more than one lighthouse were flashing far out to sea that the boat was brought to her moorings in a little rocky creek, sheltered by a reef of rocks from the Atlantic roll.

Young Grey Seal perhaps Two Weeks Old.
"I don't like this photographing business."

Grey Seals about Six Weeks Old, showing the Variation in Colouring.

A COLONY OF GUILLEMOTS.

CHAPTER V

ARDNAMURCHAN

JUTTING out into the Atlantic there stands, far removed from civilization, a wild headland. Many ships have passed it by on the sea, and their crews, maybe, have looked curiously at the grandeur and strength of its outline, but few persons have ever set foot upon its rough weather-beaten surface. On its cliffs the golden eagle has its home, and in former times the erne or sea eagle was wont to nest on its inaccessible ledges. On quiet days of early spring ravens sail and tumble above its rocks, and one may hear the shrill, mournful cry of the buzzard as she leaves her eyrie. Near by is the haunt of the wild cat, now a fast vanishing species in the Highlands, and as early as February she has been known to produce her young in the rocky cairns above the reach of the waves.

It is, I think, on the wildest of winter days that the grandeur of the headland is most apparent. Is not its very name Ardnamor-chuan—"The Point of the Ocean"? And indeed, the sea which thunders on its rocks at tide-level—rocks worn smooth by centuries of hammering—is sometimes tremendous. Due westwards the long and narrow island of Coll does little to break the great strength of the Atlantic rollers, while north of west, except perhaps Barra Head, there is no land between the rocks and America.

The tide runs fast past the point, and when the ebb of the "springs" sets in southwards against a full gale of south-west wind the spray of the breakers is carried far over the highest point of the rocks, and the deep booming roar can be heard even on the Island of Mull.

The Land of the Hills and the Glens

Though situated on the mainland of Scotland the promontory and the district around it are, curiously enough, inaccessible except from the Island of Mull. Twice weekly during the years of the war the sturdy mail-boat crossed from Tobermory to the small crofting community of Kilchoan, and was met by a ferry-boat, manned by experts who succeed in putting out to sea when it would seem as though no craft of her size could live in such weather. Often of a winter's morning I have seen, from the mail-boat, the lamp of the ferry-boat guiding the steamer to her side, at a time when even the first streaks of dawn were not yet visible in the eastern sky, and when the frosty air was clear and still.

It is only very gradually that the hand of spring—always backward in these northern latitudes—asserts itself here. On the high hills lying behind the promontory, as late as May snow still lies, deep and unbroken, but at sea level even at dead of winter it remains only for a few hours on end, and by early April, on the narrow ledges of the cliff, the grasses, browned by the salt-laden gales from off the Atlantic, have become once again tinged with green. By then, the herons have taken up their quarters on the bushes growing on the steep cliff, and are busily occupied with their broods. And with the coming of the fine weather the sea is no longer desolate as during the winter months.

One morning of early May, when the sun is warming the waters of the ocean from out a cloudless sky, and when not the faintest breeze ruffles the surface of the waters, it is seen that the ocean is peopled with many birds. As far as the eye can reach, puffins, swimming closely together in pairs, give life and activity to the water's surface. They have but just completed their long journey northward from the southern waters of the Atlantic where they have passed the winter, and have not yet gathered at their nesting grounds. With them, but each species keeping to themselves, are other members of the tribe of

22

the sea-divers, such as razorbills and guillemots. Thus the sea welcomes her bird population, which makes its home here during the fine summer months of the year.

Later, when summer has indeed come, and when day after day of brilliant sunshine has melted the snow cap from even the highest hills, companies of guillemots can be seen, flying in long strings just above the water's surface, and making their way rapidly towards the Sound of Mull. I have often wondered what takes them on this journey. It may be that they have their nesting cliffs on the islands to the nor'ard; on Eigg, maybe, or on Canna, and that they are travelling to the Lismore country to fish. Through that narrow channel of the sea lying between Duart Point on the Island of Mull, and Lismore Island, the tide runs with the strength of a river in full spate, and here is the happy fishing ground of the sea birds. During any day in the months of summer, birds of all kinds may be seen here, busy at their fishing. Sea swallows in their hundreds hover like drifting snowflakes over the tide, plunging rapidly in after the small fry which swim near to the surface. Manx shearwaters, perhaps the most graceful of our sea birds, ride buoyant on the tide, and when disturbed take wing with extreme grace of motion. How unlike the clumsy cormorant! They rise like feathers from the water, and wheel and skim in rapid flight, "banking" steeply over until their long wings graze the water, and showing to the full the poetry of flight.

Built at a height of perhaps seventy feet above the level of the high spring tides, and standing out at the extreme point of Ardnamurchan is the lighthouse, known to every sailor by reason of the brilliance of its white, steady light. On dark nights of winter, when the wind, backing to the south-east and increasing in force with each hour, sends drifting clouds scudding low across the sky, then it is that even from the distant Island of Tiree the glare of the light can be seen reflected in the stormy sky, and to the islanders the showing of this far-distant beacon is a sure portent of coming storm.

But however hard it may blow from the east of south, the gale is rarely of long duration, and perhaps even before daybreak a full westerly gale is tearing in from the sea. And for days the storm may continue from this quarter, so that the full force of the Atlantic hurls itself against the lighthouse, and from the low sunken rocks to the westward—known to seamen as the Cairns of Coll—vast columns of smoke-like spray are seen to rise, and even the biggest ships lurch past like drunken things.

Such is the restless spirit of the wild Hebridean Ocean, and it is, I think, in winter that one feels the charm of the sea at its height, and that, penetrating to the more inland districts and passing that season surrounded by even the wildest and most beautiful hills and glens, one realizes with curious strength how something is lacking here, and can understand how those bred within the sound of the Atlantic surge feel the impelling force of the mystic power of the ocean, and so often return to their sea-girt cliffs and islands in the autumn of their lives.

CHAPTER VI

THE ARCTIC SKUA AND ITS NESTING

A LONG and narrow Hebridean island. Full open to the salt spray of the Atlantic, a few small hills and granite rocks alone offer any shelter from the storm, and it is rare that the boom of the surf may not be heard throughout the length and breadth of the island. Here it was that I first learnt to know the Arctic skua at the time of its nesting.

It is not until the very end of May, when most of the gulls have hatched out their young, that the skuas reach their nesting-grounds from their southern winter quarters —for none of their tribe winters in the British Isles. Indeed, as late as the first week in June I have seen them, in pairs, haunting the sandy shores of an island to the south'ard of the one on which they nest, evidently on their way to the nesting-grounds, and by the 15th of that month some of the nests are still incomplete.

It is on the north end of the island that the Arctic or Richardson's skuas—for the species possesses two names— make their home during the months of summer sunshine. Their nesting-ground is a desolate stretch of boggy moorland. Here and there lochans lie hidden away in the hollows, and here also is the haunt of the tribe of the speckled trout, and of the red-throated diver.

It was a wonderful morning of mid-June that I first visited the nesting-ground of the skua gulls. Not the faintest of breezes blew in from the Atlantic, not a single cloud relieved the deep blue of the sky. So quiet was the surface of the sea that the course of every current could clearly be seen, while away in the distance the big hills of the Isle of Mull, and behind them again, of the Lochaber

country, were wonderfully clear. As the keeper—a keen
ornithologist—and I traversed the uneven ground of the
bog, a curlew, by her oft-repeated alarm calls, showed us
that she had a family somewhere in the neighbourhood—
an interesting discovery to us, for hitherto the curlew had
not been known to breed on the island. The heat was
intense, and many species of blood-sucking flies, some of
them resplendent in gorgeous hues, made things unpleasant.
Weeks of heat and drought had shrunken the lochans until
they had left a dark oozy rim around their shores, and over
the bogs one could to-day walk dryshod.

Herring and lesser black-backed gulls were nesting on
the rocky knolls, and on the margins of the small lochs
were colonies of graceful common gulls. At length, sail-
ing in circles with the tribe of the gulls, but rather above
them, and showing much grace and power in their flight,
a pair of skua gulls passed overhead.

And now, from the top of a knoll, one looked down
upon a level piece of boggy moorland, with a lochan in
the background on which the strong sunshine sparkled.
This was the haunt of the Arctic skua. Mingled with the
cries of the gull colonies which were nesting near, and
which we had disturbed, came call-notes far more shrill
and long-drawn, uttered by the skuas as they flew rest-
lessly round us. I think the skua gull, or "Croma rithe-
achar," as it is known in the Gaelic—is almost unique in
its habit of feigning injury in order to deceive the in-
truder while yet its eggs are freshly laid. Many birds
do this after the hatching of their young, and some
even when the eggs are hard set, but I can recall
no other bird which practises this deception so early in
its nesting. Both the cock and hen skuas would circle
above their nest with apparent indifference, and then would
alight together on some knoll two or three hundred yards
away, or even farther, where they would stand beating
their wings helplessly as though wounded. Indeed, so

wary were they that I did not once see a bird rise from her eggs, and, acting on the keeper's advice, we both took up our positions on a small hill overlooking the nesting-ground, and waited there for the colony to return to their eggs. I do not ever remember a hotter day, and the "cleg" flies, which had been troublesome even while we walked, became infinitely more so as we remained stationary. It is one of the drawbacks of the kilt that any biting insect finds an excellent field for its labours in the vicinity of one's knees, and it must be confessed that the Highlander is on such occasions at a distinct disadvantage to the Sassenach.

Although such light sitters, the skuas soon returned to their nests, apparently ignoring our presence, and settled down to brood. The colony was of no very great extent, and I should doubt if there were more than two dozen pairs at the outside, probably fewer. Immediately we stood up, every bird rose from her nest, but one I marked down, and after a good deal of searching discovered her secret. The nest, if such it could be called, was a slight depression scraped amongst the heather and grasses, and contained one dark egg, of much the colour of the egg of the black-headed gull, only larger. During the time I was photographing it the birds did not come near, and in order to find a second nest we had again to retire to the hill-top and watch once more. The second nest we found, contained two eggs, of lighter colour than the one first discovered. For a while we stayed at the nesting-ground, watching the skuas in their fine powerful flight as they sailed and wheeled high overhead, their forked tails rendering them conspicuous from the gulls, even apart from their cries and flight.

As we sat there, at first no craft of any kind showed on the sea, but at length from out the shadows of Mull a small herring drifter could be seen through the glass, making for the island. Very slowly she neared us, and then, from the Sound of Mull a buoyant-floating yacht approached and passed us by.

With the coming of the evening there sprang up a breeze from the north, so that the sun as it sank towards the north-western horizon shed its rays on many small sparkling waves.

And so we left the home of the skua for that day, and made our way back to the small settlement lying at the head of the only sea loch and anchorage which the island possesses.

About a week later I was again on the island, and hoped to have the opportunity of obtaining photographs of the skua at home. The peaty ground of the nesting site made it easy to dig out a "hide," the sides of which were constructed of the turf which had been removed in the excavations. The roof was made of a number of sticks laid across and resting on either side, and on these again were placed more squares of turf to hide the wood. A hole was left in front of the hide, and the camera was placed here in such a way that even the lens was out of sight, whilst it dominated the nest. In the making of the hide the keeper was full of useful suggestions—indeed, had it not been for his help the photographs which illustrate this chapter could never have been taken. Our first day's work consisted in starting the building of the hide, which we left before it had reached too large dimensions in case the skuas should forsake their nest. The next morning we again made our wearisome tramp to the nesting-ground, and, having found the birds still in possession, were not long in completing the erection. A piece of canvas, which we rubbed with peat in order to render it more in harmony with its surroundings, served as a door, and on my entering the hide the keeper shut me in and, as far as possible, hid the canvas with pieces of turf. The inside of the hide was not really uncomfortable as such places go, but it was extraordinarily wet, though, as the weather was uniformly hot and sunny, this was no hardship.

Arctic Skua Approaching her Eggs.

Arctic Skua on her Nest.

ARCTIC SKUA ON THE NEST CALLING TO ITS MATE.

The Arctic Skua and its Nesting

Having, then, seen me safely concealed in my hiding-place, the keeper retired to the knoll from where we had first watched the birds, and with camera carefully focused on the nest I waited anxiously the return of the skua. I had not long to wait, for quite fearlessly the hen bird—for such I took her to be—circled once or twice above the nesting-ground and then alighted gracefully a short distance from her eggs. One of the photographs illustrating this chapter shows her as she stood immediately before settling down on to her nest.

An extremely interesting point in birds of the skua tribe is the fact that they have two distinct varieties of plumage. Some birds have the neck and breast white, while in others these parts are of a dark sooty brown. In the case of the pair I had under observation the hen had the breast dark and the cock had this part of his plumage white.

For perhaps an hour I remained in the hide, and secured a number of photographs. I had anticipated a difficulty in changing the plates, but managed to do this without disturbing my "sitter." When I wished to leave my hiding-place, being unwilling to betray my presence in the erection, I crept to the "door," and by waving a handkerchief attracted the keeper's notice. Immediately he stood up the skua sprang from her nest and vanished from my restricted view.

That afternoon, in the house of the local postmaster—who was also a keen photographer—I developed my plates, and decided to cross over to the nesting-ground next day to make some further efforts.

When morning broke the sky was still cloudless, but a gale from the north swept the island. From a rocky plateau one could see the big waves breaking in on the shore, and the sun shone on an expanse of turbulent waters. The nesting-ground of the skua was in comparative shelter, and beyond causing the hide to vibrate a little, the wind did not affect me. I was, as before, seen safely into the structure by

The Land of the Hills and the Glens

my friend the keeper and exposed several plates on my
"sitter." On settling down, she invariably shuffled her egg
well underneath her, with the characteristic motion used, I
think, by all birds when sitting. Sometimes she appeared to
be bored and would yawn, then close her eyes and indulge in
a short nap. Her mate usually circled overhead, and even
above the wind I could clearly hear his shrill, powerful cry.
Once she answered him, and I was fortunately able to "snap"
her with her mouth wide open as she called.

The same afternoon I returned to the spot without the
keeper, and crept into the hide, but although I waited in
my hiding-place a long time the skua never summoned up
sufficient courage to return to her nest, remaining, together
with her mate, standing some fifty yards away. This, I
think, proved what has often been asserted, namely that the
majority of birds cannot, or at all events, do not, count more
than one. That is, if two people walk up to the hide, and
if, after a few minutes one of them moves away it never seems
to occur to the birds that the other conspirator is inside,
whereas if only one man appears at the nesting site and he
enters the hide and does not leave it, the birds realize that
he must be inside, so do not return, however long or quietly
he may wait.

It is well on to mid July before the first of the young
skuas are hatched. Clad in dark down, they run actively
almost from the start and do not long remain in the nest.
At this time their parents range far and wide to provide
them with food, and I have often watched them winging
their way home across the sea of an evening, and have
marvelled at the beauty and strength of their flight, and how
they make light of a breeze of a force sufficient to worry
even the most powerful of the gulls.

The skua is, indeed, the pirate of the seas, and a strong
and dashing pirate he is too. For the most part he makes
his living by robbing sea birds of their rightful prey. Indeed,
one of his Gaelic names is Fascadeir, or "Squeezer." Those

30

The Arctic Skua and its Nesting

birds he most persecutes are the tribe of the terns. A skua will take up his station at the water's edge on, maybe, a sandy beach from which terns and gulls are fishing. The pirate seems to be dozing and is unheeded by the other birds, one of which, near him, captures a fish too large for it to swallow at once. Like a flash, the skua rises, and relentlessly pursues his victim until the latter in terror drops its catch, which the freebooter seizes before it has fallen to the water. Even a bird of such command of flight as the tern very rarely indeed succeeds in getting away from a skua, that is to say, with its fish still in its possession.

There is an interesting tradition regarding the skua in the Hebrides. It is said that a former Lord MacDonald was on his way by boat to Uist, and a big storm arose. When near his destination a great sea almost overwhelmed his boat, and two birds, a skua and a gull, were seen to be engaged in combat in the air above the ship. The one was "Yellow Claws," daughter of Donald, son of Cormas, the other was "Hump-backed Blue-eye" from Cracaig. Both birds were celebrated witches in disguise. The former was endeavouring to sink the boat while the latter was attempting to save it, and was successful, for Lord MacDonald arrived safely at his destination.

As soon as the young skuas are strong enough for the journey south, both young and old leave their nesting quarters, and set out for more southerly latitudes. At times they are driven from their course by continued gales, and large numbers may then be seen making their way southwards across inland districts. As a rule, however, they travel by sea, or along the coastline.

The Arctic skua is not known as a nesting species in either England or Ireland—though found in one or two districts on the mainland of Scotland as well as on certain Hebridean islands and the Orkneys and Shetlands.

CHAPTER VII

THE BIG GLEN

IN the Island of Mull, noted for its wild hill scenery and the beauty of its deep valleys, is the glen of which I write. It is known as the Glen More, or "Great Glen"—for does it not traverse the whole breadth of the island from seashore to seashore?—and during a sojourn on this western island I learned to know it intimately, and appreciate fully its wildness and charm.

Few people pass through the glen, even during the long summer days, and during the winter months, when dark mist-clouds brood constantly on the hills, the rough road leading through it is untrodden for days on end.

During winter, too, great gales from the south-west and west, sweeping straight from off the surface of the broad Atlantic, sigh and moan through the glen, driving before them stinging showers of sleet and rain, so that it is almost impossible to walk against the storm, and the glen is filled with gloom and stern grandeur.

The raven has his home in the glen. On still days, when the hills are purple, and when the view is wide and clear, one can hear him croaking huskily from afar, and can see him, accompanied maybe by his mate, forging his way with powerful wing-beats to some far-off rock where he has his nest.

The eagle formerly bred in the glen, and even without leaving the track one can see the small rock where, overlooking a dark loch—Loch Airdglas—the hen bird brooded her two speckled eggs in early spring. Now the rock is taken over by a pair of ravens and the eagle has gone. Buzzards there are in plenty in the glen. How closely

MARCH SNOWS IN THE FOREST.

STAGS IN THE BIG GLEN AT EVENING.

do these birds resemble the eagle! They soar in similar fashion, circling high above the hillsides, and they plane rapidly against the wind. But there is one thing they sometimes do which marks them at once from the eagle, that is, they hover like some great kestrel above that part of the hillside where they have seen a young rabbit, or maybe a mouse, disappear.

During the hour after sunset, in the months of May or June, hurried, purring notes sometimes break the quiet of the glen. Notes quite unlike those of any other bird; but maybe the "singer" is seen seated on some old post, and then he can be identified as the elusive night-jar, or goatsucker as he is often called—a bird rarely seen during the hours of daylight, and a summer migrant only to the glen. One of the last of the summer visitors to arrive, it is far on in May before his calls are heard, and then one can be assured that summer is at length come.

The wild hyacinth grows in the glen. In late May, when the sun shines strongly and the last of the northerly winds of spring has passed by, the glen is tinged with blue, and the quiet air of an evening is laden with the sweet scent of countless of these fragile flowers. Far up the hillsides the hyacinths are to be found; they approach even the ptarmigan country and the land of the eagle.

The glen is noted for its grazing. During a summer that is past a magnificent growth of grass stretched through the strath from one end to the other. Even during the opening days of September the glen was still as green as in midsummer, but soon a succession of winds from the north brought great cold for the season of the year, and from green the grasses turned to red and brown, showing up, some of them, like flaming patches against the dark hill faces.

Many deer are in the glen. During the summer days, when the sun rides high in the heavens, and when it is good to live, I have seen the stags gathered in groups on

D

some rocky point overlooking the glen, whither they had gone to feel the cool sea breeze moving gently up to them. There they have remained almost motionless for hours on end, and not until the sun was dipping westward have they moved down to graze on the fresh grass at the burnside. At the head of the glen, just on the watershed, is a hill face with southern exposure where deer—stags and hinds—are to be seen grazing almost every day of winter and early spring. The hillside is a warm one, and snow rarely covers it, so pasture may be sought there when snow and ice are holding fast in their grip the north-facing slopes. In the height of summer deer are rarely seen in the glen, but during September nights, when the world is still, when the earth has not as yet lost her summer freshness, and when the moon is high in the heavens, I have seen the ghostly forms of stags cross the track before me, and have heard their roaring echoing from hill to hill.

On a clear day one sees far from the glen. There is one point where, through a dip in the hills, Ben Cruachan, that hill which rises so steeply above Loch Awe, arrests the eye. Often I have watched the setting sun striking full on its conical top, transforming the whole hillside to gold, and lighting up the lingering beds of snow in its glow. Frequently in hot summer weather Cruachan is covered with dark thunder-clouds, while in the glen of which I write the sun shines warm and clear; for thunder rarely comes to these island hills during the summer months, though during winter, gales from west or north-west bring many thunderstorms in from the wild sea which breeds them.

There are two burns in the glen. One flows towards the east; the other—reached after the watershed has been crossed—to the west, and to the open Atlantic. Near the head of the glen a chain of hill lochs store the water, and with the first spate of July many grilse and sea trout—a few salmon among them, too—enter the burn from the sea and move rapidly up to these hill lochans. On a calm day one sees many trout breaking the surface of the loch, and a solitary cormorant may often be spied—for I feel sure it is the same bird—perched on a stone near the middle of the loch, digesting a heavy meal of fish.

Curlew haunt the loch during spring and summer days. In June, when rain has fallen and refreshed the land, their vibrating and melancholy notes carry far—and there is no call so plaintive or so charming as that of the curlew—the birds sailing downwards from a height, calling all the while, till they alight at their feeding grounds at the loch's edge.

Three miles from the mouth of the burn is a deep fall-pool where the salmon pause awhile before pressing up the linn above it. Here in the small hours of a midsummer morning, when the air is altogether still and every blade of grass saturated with dew, many fine fish are caught by the angler who is ready to forgo his night's rest. For a number of years now—as far back as 1886 I heard of her nest being there—a water ouzel has built in a niche of rock bathed by the spray of the falls, and, on a heather-clad ledge near the tail of the pool, a pair of ring ouzels rear their young with the murmur of the waters ever in the ears of the mother bird as she broods her eggs.

A lonely shepherd's house stands near the linn, remote from civilization, and often have I passed the shepherd tramping the hill. On Sundays he may sometimes be seen wearing the kilt—I mention this because the national dress has so nearly disappeared from the Highlands, so that it is always a pleasure to see it nowadays—and the glen is the very place where one would expect to find it worn. His district is a wide one, and he goes to the hill in all weathers; when the rain brings down every mountain burn in spate, and when drifting snow out of the frozen north sweeps blindly across the high ground.

At the western end of the glen, where the land opens

out and the distant waters of the ocean can be seen spark-
ling in the sunlight beneath, stands the dwelling of a
stalker. In the dead of winter, when the hills are covered
in unbroken snow and frosts hold the low ground,
many deer gather, at the close of day, outside his house.
The grass is thick and fresh here—even in January I have
seen it green—and at times the stags receive a portion of
maize from the stalker's hands. At this season of the year,
deer, when hand fed, are quite fearless, and one stag used
to follow the stalker's small daughter with such persist-
ence, and his attentions became so wearying, that one day
a bucket of water thrown over him taught him, for a time
at all events, that there is a limit to the patience of even
the most kind-hearted human.

It was on a wild and stormy evening in mid-autumn that
I crossed through the glen for the last time for a season.
For many days heavy rain had fallen steadily. The burns
were big, and were rising; but as I passed, along with a
companion who also loved the glen, through the birch
wood and emerged to the open moor, the air was still.
Mist hung low on the hills, and even below the mist line
the quickly falling rain rendered their appearance blurred
and indistinct. Towards dusk, ahead of us appeared a
thick white cloud approaching from the west, and as it
reached us it brought with it a westerly wind, at first
faint, but quickly increasing till it blew with the strength
of a gale.

Even the smallest watercourses were running full to the
brim. From out the mist-cap dozens of such white streaks
of water poured down the hillsides, and the rushing sound
of the waters mingled with that of the wind. And yet,
though the spate was unusually heavy, the water of the
burns remained as clear as during the finest summer days,
for the hills here are rocky, and no peat discolours the
water even during the greatest flood. It was dark before
we reached the western end of the glen. The tide was high

A FINE HILL STAG.

In the Heart of the Hill Country.

Looking Westward across the Forest : The Mists gathering cn the Distant Hill.

The Big Glen

—higher than for many months—and the sea was heavy, so that one could see the surf breaking on the rocks out of the gloom and mist. The hills were invisible. Even their outlines were hidden by the blackness, and all through the night the rain continued to fall in fierce blasts.

And so we gave over the glen into the keeping of its own hills and left it, the home of many pleasant memories, with hearts that were sad at the parting.

CHAPTER VIII

THE LIFE OF A PTARMIGAN

RISING steeply from the Sound of Mull, and overlooking its quiet waters, is the hill known to the Gael as "Dun da Ghaoithe," or, translated into English, the Hill of the Two Winds. Few birds of any kind live their lives on its wind-scarred slopes, but around the summit cairn two or three—I do not think so many as half a dozen—pairs of ptarmigan have their haunt.

To a certain extent, I think, the ptarmigan of the western coast differ in their habits from those which have their home on the lonely plateaux of the Cairngorm Hills. In the latter district they may be counted in their hundreds, but within the sound of the Atlantic they are met with only as stragglers. It is as though they were the last outposts of the race, living in a country scarcely suited to them, and maintaining a bare existence only. In these western hills of the Island of Mull ptarmigan have many enemies. The raven is often on the Hill of the Two Winds, and many gulls of a summer's day sail backward and forward over the high ground, on the eager look out for eggs. Then there is the grey crow, that arch egg-stealer; and the golden eagle and peregrine often visit the hill. But one enemy of the ptarmigan is not present here—namely, the hill fox—for curiously enough he is unknown on Mull at the present day, though a couple of hundred years ago he seems to have lived on the island.

The lot of the ptarmigan on the Hill of the Two Winds cannot in winter be a pleasant one. The climate here is far different from that prevailing in their home in central Scotland. There the white grouse live in snow from

The Life of a Ptarmigan

November until May, while on the western seaboard the hilltops are snowbound only at occasional intervals during the months of winter. But day after day there sweeps in from the sea the mist-laden wind from the west, so that for weeks on end the hills are shrouded in cloud. The rainfall, too, is far greater than on the Cairngorms, and considerably exceeds one hundred inches in the course of the year.

In short, the ptarmigan of the Cairngorms exist under conditions more nearly approaching—though indeed noticeably different from—a continental climate, than do their cousins who cling to the wind-swept hills of the Atlantic.

The most striking characteristic of these ptarmigan of the west is, I think, the silence of the cock birds during the nesting season. Whereas on the Cairngorms these birds almost invariably utter their snorting croak when the intruder disturbs them in the vicinity of their nests, I never once, on the Mull hills on which the species breed, heard them utter any sound. Again, in the central Scottish plateaux, a ptarmigan when brooding her eggs—and even before incubation is far advanced—is an extraordinarily close sitter. Often she will allow one to approach within a foot or two of her without rising, and even when she does leave her eggs she flutters only a short distance and watches anxiously. But in Mull the birds whose nests I came across rose from their eggs in the same manner as grouse do, and vanished at top speed over the hillside, nor did I see them again. In no case was the cock near at hand—as I had usually found in the Cairngorms—to rise suddenly and accompany the hen with cheering croak.

These facts are, I think, worth setting down, for they may in part account for the ptarmigan barely holding their own on these Atlantic-girt hills. The birds undoubtedly have need of the greatest care on behalf of their eggs and young, for in no part of Scotland can their winged enemies be so numerous as in this western island. Gulls of many species, and bands of grey crows, are searching every part of the hill in fine weather, and a nest left unattended must speedily lose its eggs. It is a well-known fact that in wild stormy weather ptarmigan are restless and unapproachable, whilst on calm days it is at times impossible to make them take wing at all, so it would be of interest to know whether the prevalence of wind and storm along the western seaboard may not account for their habitual wariness there.

It is a curious experience to one who knows well the haunts beloved of the ptarmigan to search for hours among the corries of, say, Ben More Mull, and not to see a single one of these birds, nor to hear their cry. I remember that the first time I crossed that hill I saw but one bird, a cock. He was reluctant to rise, and I felt sure that he must have a sitting mate near, yet when he did take wing he flew off in silence, and continued unswervingly on his way until he had crossed over the skyline—not the usual behaviour of a ptarmigan whose sitting mate is near by. I searched, nevertheless, every foot of the ground, spending hours in the neighbourhood, but I saw nothing to lead me to suspect that a hen ptarmigan had her nest near.

As regards the time of their nesting, I think this is, perhaps, a few days earlier than on the Cairngorms, but there is little difference. A point of interest is the fact that on these western hills ptarmigan habitually live at a considerably lower level than on the Cairngorms. There it is worth while recording the fact if one of their nests is found below the three thousand foot contour line, whereas in the Island of Mull I doubt if any "tarmachan" nest at this height—the highest hill on the island is less than 3,200 feet—and the majority of the birds rear their broods at a height of from 2,500 to 2,200 feet; in some cases even lower.

I have wondered whether the ptarmigan of the Island of Mull live on the same hill from one year's end to another, or whether they may at times cross over to some of the nearer hills of the mainland, to Cruachan, perhaps, or to the high tops of the Lochaber country, where their tribe is

The Life of a Ptarmigan

more numerous than on this island. I know that in Aberdeenshire they have been seen to leave one hill and make for another across the valley of the Dee, but that was when greatly persecuted by shooters, and so I doubt whether any one of these Mull ptarmigan has ever set foot on the mainland.

A factor which may, perhaps, in part account for the scarcity of ptarmigan in the west is the almost complete absence of cranberry and blaeberry plants and of heather, on the higher reaches of the hills. It is well known how eagerly ptarmigan feed on the berries of these hill plants, and I have watched them feeding with relish on the tender shoots of the heather during winter snow in that well-known haunt of theirs the Larig Ghruamach, that remote high-lying pass connecting the headwaters of the Dee with the valley of the Spey; and blaeberry stems, as well as the fruit they love.

But when the weather is fine, and the sun shines clear on the hillside and deep sea loch, the ptarmigan of the west have from their lofty country a prospect of unsurpassed grandeur, for they exist on high and exposed ground where no other bird can face the winter storms.

It is said that the letter P in their name was inserted by the French—for what reason I know not—and that the word is originally derived from the Gaelic *Tarmach*, meaning "to be the source of" and given, perhaps, to this hill dweller as it was thought that from this bird originated all feathered life.

I remember, one day of midsummer, seeing a ptarmigan's nest within a few yards of the topmost cairn of the Hill of the Two Winds, and could not but remark on the wonderful panorama which was laid out before the sitting bird, had she the eye to see it. Two thousand five hundred feet beneath her, and so close that one might imagine a thrown stone might reach thus far, lay the deep blue waters of the Sound of Mull. No Atlantic swell disturbs these hill-girt waters,

41

but even in the finest of days a breeze draws down through the Sound—usually from the north-west—ruffling the waters and sending white-capped wavelets to break against its shingly shores. Many ships passing through the Sound would the ptarmigan see without rising from her eggs. So close below her is the sea that the glint of the wings of many terns, eager in their fishing, would be plain to her, and she would wonder, maybe, as to what tribe they might belong. From the grassy corrie beneath, the cry of the curlew would sometimes come of a quiet summer's night, and the cheery song of the wheatear, as he perched among the rocks, would be often in her ears. The eagle she would sometimes see, soaring in the teeth of a stiff breeze along the ridge above the rocks, or in calm sunny weather sailing in great circles on motionless wings above the corrie. During fine weather also the eagle would sit for hours on the cairn, digesting his meals, and throwing up fur and bones in pellets. At such times, so close would be her enemy, the ptarmigan would crouch in terror low on her nest, lest the eagle should observe her with his keen glance. On other days the eagle would be hunting, maybe, amongst the Morvern Hills, and his place on the cairn would be taken by a raven of grim aspect, preening his feathers contentedly and ultimately dozing in the strong sunshine.

At times stags would cross the hilltop, their rapidly growing horns massive looking by reason of their thick covering of velvet, and of an evening hinds would lead their young calves that way.

Hill flowers would grow near her nest. In the hot sun the blossoms of the cushion pink would throw out their sweet scent into the still air, and there would be violets, and wild pansies and the small white flowers of the mountain saxifrage, growing where the rocks are damp.

In clear weather hill upon hill would stand out of the early morning mist. South'ard, away past Duart and the Island of Lismore, would rise the twin peaks of Cruachan,

Early Morning in the Ptarmigan Country.

Ptarmigan Chick about a week old.

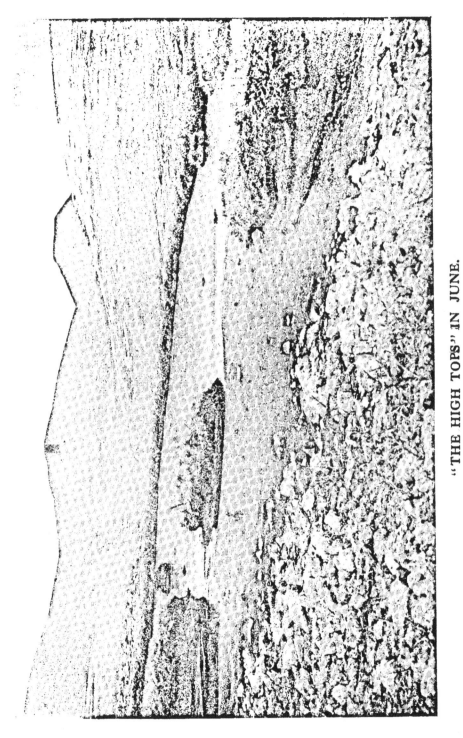

"THE HIGH TOPS" IN JUNE.

Lingering Snowfields are seen on the left of the Photograph.

The Life of a Ptarmigan

near four thousand feet high. And then to the east the ptarmigan's eye would, maybe, look along the quiet waters of Loch Linnhe to where they reached the Lochaber country, and there, shutting out all further view, she would see Ben Nevis, the greatest of Scottish hills. Always in June there would be great snowfields covering the upper reaches of that mountain, and for days on end the ptarmigan would look upon the hill deep under a fresh coating of snow —for it is a rare season indeed that the month of roses does not bring to Ben Nevis at least one heavy snowfall. Then she would see the conical hills of Glencoe—the scene of the great and never-to-be-forgotten massacre of a Scottish clan— and the high tops of the Black Mount forest where ptarmigan in numbers have their home.

But the fine weather would soon end, and there would come days when rain and mist would sweep the hilltop, and with the lifting of the mist many burns would be seen streaming down the hillsides of Morvern, to where the hills drop sheer to the waters of the Sound of Mull. And here at such times a wonderful sight would be seen—the force of the wind of so great strength that the burns would not be permitted to fall in cascades to the sea as is their wont, but the waters, caught upon the gale, would be hurled backwards in clouds of spray. I have indeed seen these hills, after heavy rain, when their waters, upward carried by the wind, had all the appearance of the smoke of many heather fires rising, and they have before now been mistaken for such.

And then on dark nights the ptarmigan, were she awake, would see the lights of passing ships, and also the flashing beacon on Eilean Glas, and the steady orange glare of the stout lighthouse on Lismore.

And so, as she brooded her richly speckled eggs, she would have much to occupy her. Yet I doubt if she saw any of these things, or if indeed so, whether they were anything to her. But one dark shape I know she recognized, and trembled for her life as the eagle passed her by at his hunting.

43

CHAPTER IX

IONA AND ITS SOUND

AWAY to the westward of the Island of Mull, and separated from the Ross by a mile of sea, there lies the small grassy island of Iona. For its size—it extends in length some three miles and is in breadth not over a mile and a half—it is perhaps the most famous island of Scotland; for here it was that Saint Columba made his landing after setting forth from Ireland in the sixth century in order to spread abroad the Christian faith.

For many years the saint had his home on the island, blessing it, so that in time it was looked upon as a spot sacred to his name and worthy of many pilgrimages.

From far lands there were brought the remains of those whose wish it was to sleep their last sleep on this holy isle Here lie the kings of many lands. No fewer than forty-eight kings of Scotland—including Macbeth—are buried here, and near them repose also kings of Ireland, Norway and Denmark. Here, too, rest great Highland chiefs whose names are bywords in Scottish history—MacLeods, Mac-Donalds, MacLeans, MacKinnons, MacQuarries—men who in olden times carried in their hands the power of life and death in their clans.

Iona's cathedral, for centuries in ruins, has now been restored, and on a clear day can be seen from afar—from Ulva's Isle, from Gometra, and from distant Treshnish.

Arising from the blessing given to the island by Columba, it is said that no serpent can survive on Iona, and I believe that on the few occasions on which adders have swum the sound they have soon perished. This immunity is also said to be found in the district of Ormsaig, in the Ross of Mull,

44

which is supposed also to have been blessed by the saint, whereas on the adjoining lands on either side adders in plenty are to be seen.

Even now one can visit a bay—Port a' churaich by name —away at the southern end of the island where are said to lie the remains of the boat which brought Columba from Ireland, and see the long grass-covered mound under which the craft was buried. Near it are many heaps of stones of various sizes, supposed to have been gathered together by the monks as penances, the heaps varying in size according to the greatness of the offence committed, and built while the monk was on his hands and knees.

Concerning the origin of the name Iona, nothing certain is known. It is said that the name, as it stood in the original Gaelic, was I-Challum-Cille, or the Island of Saint Columba. In the Gaelic of the present day " island " would be translated by " eilean," or " innis," but the " I " is said to be a shortening of the word "innis."

None, I think, who have crossed the sound on a fine day of summer will ever forget the scene, for the Sound of Iona has at all times a charm that is peculiarly its own. It may be that there yet broods here the spirit of the saint and his followers, or that the intangible influence of their personality and of the many good deeds wrought here still persists.

I shall always remember vividly the first occasion on which I crossed the sound. The season was near the shortest day, and incessant storms had swept in day after day from the Atlantic, so that the swell was strong on the rocks. But as the ferry-boat pushed out from the little harbour of Fion-phort the wind was not too fresh, and we soon covered the mile of sea and made Iona without difficulty. Toward sunset the wind veered to south-west, increasing momentarily in force, with a wild sky of green framed in black storm-clouds to windward. When the boat set sail, with every reef in, on the return passage, a gale was sweeping the waters, so that some of those in the boat—and there were many crossing

by reason of the fact that the mail-steamer had failed to call
—were of opinion that "There was no safety in the sound."
But all trusted themselves to the fine Highlander who, often
single-handed, has sailed the passage these forty years back;
and with many farewells from the shore the sail was filled and
the boat shot forward with the wind. Almost at once we were
in a heavy sea, and the wind blew with such force that all
idea of crossing to Fionphort was quickly abandoned, and,
sailing before the gale, the course was set for the sheltered
creek near the little fishing village of Kentra. Things looked
serious, for we were shipping the waves which broke white-
topped and menacing around us—the tide runs strong in the
sound, and when moving against the storm renders the swell
doubly dangerous—and each person had perforce to lie at the
bottom of the boat so that the ferryman might see the more
easily to avoid the overfalls of the heaviest waves. Some
feared that the mast would snap before the strain, but all went
well, and it was with much gratitude that we reached harbour,
and many a word of well-deserved praise and thanks did the
ferryman, soaked to the skin by the breaking waves, receive
from his Gaelic-speaking passengers.

But not always is the sound thus in winter. I have
crossed on days of February when scarce a breath of wind
ruffled the waters, when all the hills of Mull stood out clear
and blue, saving Ben More, whose summit was whitened
by snows which did not reach to the lesser peaks, and when
all the islands were clear and on Gometra every house dis-
tinct. Then there were days when a bitter north-easter,
sweeping up the waters of Loch Scridain, brought with it
from the snow-clad hills of the mainland the icy breath of
the frost spirit; when the sky over the rocks of the Wilder-
ness was of steel, and when even the Atlantic swell was
stilled by the frost. These days would perhaps come in
early spring, scorching the young grass already showing
green on Iona and numbing the early lambs with deadly
chill. But with April better weather would come to Iona

and to its sound, and there would come an end to the gales from the west and south-west—gales which on one occasion prevented the ferry-boat from crossing for a week or more, so that no inter-communication was possible between the island and the far side of the sound, though this is scarce over a mile in width.

Even before March is come the ravens on Eilean nam Ban—that island set out in the sound and breaking the force of the tide—are repairing their nest, and with each morning and evening may be seen crossing over to Fionphort as they make for their feeding ground on the Ross of Mull. In former times the red-billed chough was wont to share the rocks with them, but he has now gone; indeed, has been banished from the whole of the Hebridean coasts, and nowadays is but a fast fading memory.

And then, during fine still weather of a March month, one would see, curling from either shore of the sound, the blue smoke of the burning tangle seaweed, with pungent though pleasant smell hanging over the waters; and as April gave place to May there would be many birds amongst the rocky islands of the sound. Here would the grey crow —the "Feannaig" of the Gael—build her wool-lined nest in some niche of the rock, with a deep carpet of heather beneath to break the fall of the young should they over-balance at the nest's edge. On the pebbly beach the oyster catcher would scrape out her primitive nesting hollow and deposit therein her three speckled eggs, nor would the grey crow touch them, for it is a firm and constant law in the bird world that no individual preying by habit on its fellows shall disturb those birds nesting near it. Is it, I wonder, that they have some fellow feeling for their neighbours; or is it to secure for themselves a measure of quietness during their nesting time?

It is with the coming of May also that a new bird makes his appearance at Iona's Sound—the strong-flying solan, or the "sulair," as he is known in the Gaelic tongue. With tireless wings many of these birds, always flying singly in their hunting, patrol the sound, their cold, expressionless eyes ever searching the clear, green-tinted water for their prey, the silvery herring or the swift-swimming mackerel. They hunt in silence always, do these solans, and it is only when two birds, most intent on their fishing, all but collide in mid-air that their harsh, grating cry is heard. But at their nesting rock—on Ailsa Craig, maybe, or on lone Saint Kilda—the silent solan is quiet no longer, and during every hour of the day and night a multitude of cries arise from thousands of birds. Harsh and grating as their voices are, the solans have in them a certain charm, for one always associates them with days of summer and with the full tide of pulsating life.

The Sound of Iona is famous for its flounders. They are, so it is said, of unsurpassed flavour, and of a morning the menfolk from the little township of Kentra may be seen putting to sea and setting their long lines along the sandy bottom of the sound. I doubt if the solans take the flounders in their fishing; they would, I suspect, be a difficult mouthful to dispose of, for it must be remembered that the solan swallows his fish whole, and always bolts his catch before rising to the surface.

The fields of Iona are manured in springtime by the fronds of the laminarian seaweed, which, if the wind be favourable, are washed ashore on the western side of the island in great quantities during May. In former days it was customary, should the "barr dearg"—as the weed is known in the Gaelic—not come ashore at the usual season, and the crops were likely to be spoilt for want of the proper nourishment, to prepare on a certain Thursday in May a great cauldron of porridge, which was cast into the sea on the western side of the island as an offering to the Sea Spirit. The day of this ceremony was known in the Gaelic as "Diardaoin a' bhrochain mhoir," or "the Thursday of the big porridge."

Iona and Its Sound

Before the days of the steamers—before the time of the old and trusty steamship *Dunara Castle,* which brings to the Highlanders their provisions from the south—the people of Iona were wont, after the close of the harvest, to set out for Glasgow in their smacks, carrying with them the produce of the island. For this passage a steady northerly wind was all-important, so that before they set sail the voyagers made their way to a certain well on the island, stirred its waters—the while uttering mysterious sentences in the Gaelic, which have now unfortunately been lost—and asked the Spirit of the Well that the wind might be favourable to them. Afterwards they proceeded to another well, going through the same ceremonies here and asking for a steady and continuous south wind to bring them back to Iona. The two wells are known as "Tobar na gaoithe tuath" and "Tobar na gaoithe deas," that is, "the well of the north wind" and "the well of the south wind."

The sun shines bright on the sound these summer days, lighting up the white sands on Eilean aon Reithe—the Island of the One Ram—so that they are of a dazzling brightness and contrast strikingly with the deep lights on the water in which the blue of the sky is reflected and even appears to be intensified. The older name of this wild island is said to be "Eilean annraidh," or "the Island of Storms"—a fitting name for this sentinel guarding Iona from the hosts of the north wind.

The tribe of the sea swallows are filled these days with the joy of life, and on graceful wings are busy at their fishing from sunrise till long after sunset. But even before these birds are thinking of their nesting the ravens have already reared their young and have taken them far afield in their hunting, and in the eyrie of the peregrine, built where the cliffs rise sheer from the Atlantic, the young hawks are already losing their first downy coat and are growing their clear-cut, powerful wings.

There is one small, unobtrusive bird which makes its

E   49

equally unobtrusive and carefully concealed nest amongst the short-cropped heather fringing Iona's Sound. Known as the twite, or mountain finch, its four or five eggs are of a pale sky-blue ground colour, on which are set a few markings and spots of a very dark brown, so that the eggs are of great beauty, and rival in their colouring the unclouded summer sky. When the north wind—cold even at this season—blows for days up the sound the spray from the white-topped breakers is often carried across to the heather where the mother twite broods her eggs, but her nest is always built beyond the reach of the tide or the roughest sea. In its habits there is much that is of interest in the mountain finch. In the Hebrides and along the extreme west coast of Scotland it makes its nest usually at sea level, while in the more central districts of the country I have come across it nesting on the highest hills, where, at a height of three thousand feet and more, it has for its companion only the mist-loving ptarmigan and the silent-flying eagle.

When the midsummer sun is strong on Iona's sands, and when the crofters' cattle have sought the shelter of the cool rocks of Dun I, then it is that at times there can be seen far out at sea a white bank of mist hiding from view the distant Island of Tiree. Carried forward by the westerly breeze, the cloud approaches, and soon the white vapour covers land and sea. For a time the sun gives battle to the cloud, and now and again dispels the mist pall, but soon the fog is so thick that even the Island of Mull is blotted out. On such a summer's evening I have crossed the sound when not a breath of air ruffled the waters, and when the boil of the tide was the only thing that stirred. Gone were the solans to fish elsewhere, and as the boat was pushed out into the sound the shore faded away almost at once. Many unfortunate bumble bees, having entirely lost their bearings, flew aimlessly but hopefully towards the boat, and when they were undeceived in their expectation that

Iona and Its Sound

they had found land, lacked in some cases the strength to fly farther and fell exhausted in the water.

One island lying in the sound is noted for the white heather which grows on its narrow crown, and, indeed, on all the islands a profusion of wild flowers blossom in their season. Here there are no trees, for the great winds of winter will suffer nothing beyond the height of a bush to offer resistance to their rush.

But one island there is on which no shrub grows, on which no heather carpets the ground, and that is the lonely rock of Reidh Eilean, which lies west of the sound, west of Iona herself. The rough summit of a hill set in the Atlantic and just rising beyond the water's surface is this lonely island. Many sea birds have their home here, and of a summer's night the silvery tribe of the herring play on the surface of the quiet waters, and perhaps the storm petrel—on whose notes a piper of old composed a tune—flits swallow-like past, winging her way to those Islands where she has her home during the season of her nesting.

Guarded by her sentinel islands and her sound of restless waters, Iona, full of sacred memories, rests quietly and securely, for she is safe in the keeping of the Spirit of the West Wind, which can bring her naught but good from the vast spaces of the sea.

CHAPTER X

THE SEA POOL

IN the mist-shrouded Island of Mull, and lying in the shadow of big hills on which ptarmigan nest and the eagle has his home, is the sea pool of which I write. The small river which forms the pool has its source in a chain of lochs lying within six miles of the sea, yet its tributaries are many, and by the time the stream reaches the sea pool its waters are not unworthy of the silvery salmon, and the sea trout, exulting in its strength.

The pool is not deep—when the water is at its average height the deepest hole is not more than six feet—yet at certain seasons of the year it holds many fish in its clear waters. An average tide from the still sea loch into which the river runs does not reach it, but at the full of the "springs" the sea enters the pool, and dams back its waters so that at times they overflow the adjoining rough pastures where the green plover scream and wheel during the season of their nesting. At such times, swimming in with the salt water, many sea trout, and perhaps a few salmon also, enter and populate the pool.

The season of the fishing falls late in these parts; there is no early show of fish when the ground is still frost-bound and the hills are deep in snow: indeed July is usually more than half gone before the great "run" of salmon and sea trout ascend the river. The pool, it is true, is peopled throughout the winter by a few small sea trout or "finnock," and when the frost grips the countryside, and the pool is held firm beneath a sheet of black ice, these small fish may be seen swimming in the waters beneath, but they are not worth the taking until they have returned to the sea loch in the spring for the rich feeding that is there.

It is during the early weeks of April that the first "run" of sea trout enter the sea pool, but they are few in number and some still show the want of good feeding. One April morning that I recall was of singular charm. No breath stirred the still leafless birches from which the missel thrush uttered his melancholy song, and the air was clear and warm. There was a small freshlet in the river—just enough to make the pool of good fishing size—and the fish were there and were on the take, so that I had my first basket of the season. I well remember how a cormorant, following doubtless the run of fish, took up his quarters there in my absence, and thus rendered all further fishing useless. I think the keeper laid him low ultimately, but too late, for he spoilt the only run of spring fish that season. About this time an extraordinary sharp thunderstorm visited the glen at dusk. It is a curious fact that along the western coast these storms occur with more frequency in winter than summer, and are accompanied by a high wind—perhaps even by a gale. On this day a strong breeze from the west had brought with it squalls of hail with clear sunny intervals between them, but of thunder there was no sign, so that the storm when it suddenly burst overhead was quite unexpected. In quick succession blinding flashes of lightning lit up the hills in vivid greenish light, the thunder following on the instant. So thick was the hail that almost at once the ground was clad in white, and when after less than fifteen minutes the storm, hurried forward by the wind, passed eastward, it carried with it the season of spring and left winter in its stead.

Even though no sea trout are in the pool, it is good to sit by its banks of a fine spring day, for the lover of Nature finds many friends here. At times the air is filled with the trilling call of many curlews, and in the dusk of the evening these shy birds, absorbed in their spring song, may sail towards one and alight, almost at one's feet, still calling. And with the coming of daybreak, one is awakened by their note—a note that must always have a special charm for one who is a lover of the wild and mist-swept places—and may watch them as they come down from the hills to alight at their feeding grounds near the pool. I know the curlew and his haunts as well as most, and I can safely say that in no place have I seen and heard so many of their tribe as near the banks of this sea pool.

During March and April the cry of the green plover rings often in the ear—for do they not nest within a stone's throw of the pool?—and the flute-like calls of a pair of redshanks that with each season make their nest in the rough grass hard by carry far in the stillness of an April evening.

And then, with the coming of May, the birches of the hillside above the pool become tinged with the most delicate green, and before the soft southerly breeze they sway with feather-like motion. And from them for the first time since the summer of the past year come the clear notes of the cuckoo, and the sweet and plaintive song of the willow warbler. From them, too, the tree pipit—newly arrived from Africa—flies up perpendicularly into the blue sky, and as he sails leisurely downward to his favourite perch, utters his cheery song.

And now, the river banks welcome to themselves the sandpiper, straight from his southern winter quarters—with pleasure one hears for the first time his "wheet, wheet, wheet," as he wings his way rapidly up the water-side—and when the birches are in full leaf, and even the late-budding oaks have taken on a tinge of green, the nightjar may be heard uttering in the twilight his husky notes.

As spring gives place to summer, the hill grasses in the high corries above the sea pool, where the ptarmigan croak and the golden eagle sails on tireless wings, at length take on a tinge of vivid green, and show up brightly against the dark rocks. The sky is clear these days, and all Nature is renewed by the strong sunlight; but even in the month of June big rainstorms roll in from the Atlantic, and before the soft westerly wind the grey mists advance to the hills. It is the characteristic of the western coast that rain rarely falls unless it is accompanied by a strong breeze, so that it drives aslant through the glen almost in the form of spray. The storm continues but an hour or two before the hills run water. Water-courses which are usually dry carry to the river of the sea pool rushing torrents, and I know of no grander sight than to watch them emerge from the mist-cap, and—their murmur mingling with the rush of the wind—hurry to join the parent river beneath.

To the fisherman a June rainstorm must always bring good cheer, for do not the heaviest salmon enter the river during this month? Curiously enough, a salmon has never, I think, been taken in the sea pool itself; they hurry past, for their instinct leads them westward up to the linn and to the chain of lochs beyond. During June, few sea trout enter the river, but early in the following month they press from the Atlantic into the sea loch through the narrow channel joining it with the ocean, so that on quiet summer nights many of their race may be seen leaping in the salt water of the estuary, and the soft "plosh" of their rising carries far in the still air.

During these days of midsummer the scent of the bog myrtle is carried far over the loch, for myriads of its plants have their home in the boggy land leading down to the water. A profusion of sea thrift is now in blossom on the shingle lying near the sea pool, so that a tinge of pink is to be seen over all the river estuary. Here oyster catchers have their nests, and with lack of foresight sometimes lose their eggs with a high spring tide.

From the bushes stonechats sing and call, and with wonderful cunning hide from the intruder the whereabouts of their nests, search he never so carefully. Whinchats are here also, and no less skilled are they than their cousins in hiding the site of their delicate eggs of pale unspotted blue or their large family of sober-coloured young. In the wood of stunted oaks the young of the barn or white owl are already full-fledged in the hollow of the tree where they have been reared, and the plaintive alarm note of the wood warbler may be heard as she flutters anxiously from bough to bough in the neighbourhood of that small domed nest containing her large family of half-fledged young.

There are no hours of darkness at this time. For an hour either side of midnight twilight covers the land, but as early as one o'clock I have watched the sunrise firing the high cirri clouds in the north-eastern sky and tinging them with crimson.

For weeks, maybe, the sea trout must remain in the salt water, for even the biggest flood of midsummer runs down in a few hours, and for many days scarce a trickle of water finds its way to the sea pool. When at length the long-awaited rain comes and the river quickly rises, grand sport may be had by the fisherman who is on the spot. One such July day I recall when the mist was low, and when from out the mist-cap every hill burn rushed, full to the brim. Many sea trout were in the pool that day, and they were not above taking a nicely thrown teal and green or brown hackle, so that by evening one's basket was well filled and one heeded not the west wind that blew the rain across from the hills with gale force and soaked one to the skin.

The next day brought sunshine and showers, so that when the sun shone, hot and clear, the scent of the bell heather came across the glen from the hillside beyond the river, and mingled with it was the aroma from many bog myrtle plants.

In August the main run of fish is past, but with each "freshlet" belated sea trout enter the river and quickly ascend to the lochs. At this season the banks of the river are breast-high with the deep green bracken, and the ling under the birches is heavy with blossom, so that as one

The Sea Pool

passes one's footsteps send showers of yellow pollen to the ground. It is now that the midges are most plentiful, and I have more than once been almost compelled to leave the river bank, so violent were their onslaughts.

With September come the small sea trout or "finnocks," and the sea pool is peopled with them until the end of October, when fishing closes. These fish do not run far up the river, and many of them do not penetrate beyond the sea pool. In size they average about half a pound, and give very fine sport. I think they come best to the fly of an evening in late September, after sunset, and when the tide is just on the turn. The spring tides in these parts are at the full a little after six o'clock in the evening, and when, after damming back the pool, they recede once more, the sea trout instantly come on the take, and seem to be quite unaffected by the number of victims drawn from the pool. At such times mergansers often swim in from the sea loch and haunt the waters. Very industrious fishers are they, and it is indeed a sign of ill omen to the human angler should they rise from the pool at his approach.

An old Highland story is sometimes told of the Glen of the Sea Pool. A certain noted hunter—Ian Mor, by name—killed a fine stag in the glen and conveyed it by night to his home nearly five miles distant. In those days the fairy people—or "Sithean," as they are known in the Gaelic—played a great part in men's lives, and many charms were used to counteract their influence, which was not always beneficial. On this occasion the fairies laid an invisible weight on the stag, a common practice of theirs, and on Ian Mor confessing to his companion that he felt as though he had the house on his back, his friend stuck his knife into the deer—this was a sure charm against fairy influence—and the animal at once became immensely lighter.

With October, the last month of the fishing, there comes a keen edge to the wind, and before the advance of the frosts the bracken loses its green hue and droops listlessly to the ground. The birds have almost all gone, but the cheery stonechats will remain through the winter and the white owls will still pass in their hunting during a day of gloom, or, in fine weather, after sunset.

The river is often in spate these days and the gales are strong and frequent. Then, one morning, the hill-tops and high-lying corries bear their first covering of snow, and one realises that winter is at hand.

In the birch wood, where the trees now stand clad in gold, the big stags roar continually, for the storms have driven them down from the hills, and tribes of redwing and fieldfares cluster on the rowan berries.

And so winter comes again to the glen and to the sea pool.

CHAPTER XI

MEMORIES OF HIGHLAND STALKERS

LIVING far removed from the great cities, and often amongst all that is most admirable and grand in Nature, the Highland stalker has a certain distinctive charm of his own. In him is often set deeply the poetry and romance of his race. He has lived out his quiet life in his glen, with the big hills he knows so well sheltering his home from the fierce winter storms, and his glen is his whole world. In winter as well as in summer he is abroad in all weathers. In wild January blizzards he may be out on the high ground after hinds, and may have his work cut out to gain shelter before he is overcome by the choking drift. When it is realized how rapidly a blizzard of dry, powdery snow from the north may descend on the uplying glens, obliterating every object more than a few yards distant, it is a matter of surprise how seldom the Highland stalker does go astray during a winter's storm. Such incidents occasionally do occur, it is true, but I have never heard of a life being lost, for a stalker has a more intimate knowledge of the ground of his beat than any other man, and in summer when the mist lies thick on the hill, he is able to guide the sportsman unerringly, not only to safety, but also to that part of the ground where, with the particular wind which happens to be blowing at the time, stags are most likely to be found.

During the closing days of December, 1906, a terrific blizzard of snow swept the country without warning, save that the glass had dropped steadily, although the wind was in a northerly quarter. On the morning of December 26 the frost was intense, and there was scarcely a cloud in the sky, so that there seemed every prospect of a clear day to follow. Towards noon, however, a grey cloud appeared on the northern horizon; snow began to fall, and continued without intermission for forty-eight hours, accompanied by a whole gale from the north. A number of stalkers went to the hill on that particular morning, but though many of them had to fight hard to regain their homes, they all succeeded in reaching them safely before dark. It was, all the same, fortunate for them that the northerly wind had for some days previous to the advent of the great storm brought frost and snow squalls to the hill country, so that the hinds had left the higher grounds for the shelter of the woods of veteran Scots firs, and were thus in more accessible quarters than is usually the case.

In spring the stalker's work takes him rarely to the high ground, except, maybe, to kindle a hillside where the heather is, to his way of thinking, too long to afford the best grazing for his deer, and it is not until the latter end of August that the heaviest work of the year begins.

Day by day, before the "gentlemen" are astir, the stalker is closely scanning the corries through his glass, and day after day, perhaps under a blazing sun, with no breath of air to cool the hillsides, perhaps in a heavy storm of rain and snow, he is abroad on the high grounds.

The Highland stalker sees many a fine sight during his expeditions to the high hills. He sees, maybe, the battle between the sun and the mists, or, again, the coming of the cold north wind to the hills—the north wind which drives irresistibly the fine weather before it, and which settles down on the hill-tops, carrying with it cloud and impenetrable gloom. He sees, too, the black eagle—the "Iolaire Dubh" of the hillman—and round the eagle he weaves many stories.

Fiona Macleod related how a Highland shepherd gave

the eagle the curious name "An-t-eun mor abu." An-t-eun mor signifies the "great bird," but the shepherd was at a loss to translate the last word. Some time later Fiona Macleod was able to discover that the word "abu" was the slogan of the Gaels in earliest times.

The hill stalker admires the eagle. A veteran hillman recently told me how he "was regarding the eagle and was taking notice of the nobility of the bird" when mobbed by grey crows, the eagle continuing on its flight heedless of the repeated attacks of its small adversaries. A curious expression has on more than one occasion been used in conversation with me on the soaring of the King of Birds, the stalker observing that he had seen the eagle "waving" in the sky.

I shall long remember a pathetic story which a most benevolent looking old stalker unfolded when I met him near his home. Surrounding his house was a small clump of larch and Scots firs in which a kestrel had built her nest and reared her family. The young kestrels left the nest, but how one of the brood met an untimely death had best be narrated in the stalker's own words: "The little haak, I saw him on a tree, so I said to him, ' Come down, man,' and he came down and I killed him with a stick." The story is a humorous one, but has its pathetic side. One can imagine the scene. The small kestrel, tired maybe, and resting after its first flight, the appearance of the enemy, and the regrettable tragedy.

I remember once when on the hill, a white-bearded stalker asking me whether I could name to him the Seven Sleepers of the Earth. I learnt from him later that he considered without doubt that the wheatear, or stonechacker, as he called it, was one of the seven, and he treated my scepticism with something like pity. As a conclusive proof of his statement, he described to me how he had on one occasion discovered a hibernating wheatear at the end of a hole on an exposed moor. His story was evidently true, but the weight of the assertion was lessened when he added that the bird was found in the month of March. It would thus appear that this wheatear was an early migrant which had arrived prematurely in the Highlands, and which had sought refuge at the end of a burrow from the cold spell which prevailed at the time.

Though I have met many stalkers during my wanderings on the hills, I much doubt whether the place can ever be filled of a noted hillman who has now been laid to rest near the corries he knew and loved so well. It could indeed be said of this veteran that he was one of Nature's most perfect gentlemen. The giant hills of his glen he knew as well as any man, and many were the interesting sights he had witnessed when out on his expeditions. On one occasion he had followed a wounded stag to where it had fallen in a burn, and as he was engaged in "gralloching" the beast, he heard an object strike the water beside him with a splash. In surprise, he raised himself quickly—to see a golden eagle check itself suddenly on its downward stoop and soar upwards, leaving a dead ptarmigan to float down stream.

On another occasion the stalker was on the high tops during a fine summer day. Ptarmigan were restless, and soon the cause of this restlessness was evident, for a couple of eagles crossed the hill, flying out beyond a steep face and passing, if anything, a trifle below the level at which the stalker sat. The "tarmachan" flew wildly, aimlessly, in all directions, but the leading eagle, choosing a victim, rapidly overhauled the bird and struck it down.

The stalker had also watched the eagles teach their young to fly, sailing out from the rocky hillside and using every persuasion to induce their youngsters to follow them, until at last their efforts were rewarded, and each eaglet, swaying and rocking as an aeroplane in a whole gale of wind, soared out over the corrie.

Not so long ago I was lucky enough to come across a

Memories of Highland Stalkers

cairngorm stone of somewhat exceptional size while out on the high hills, and though the stalker rarely allowed his feelings to become evident, in this instance he was constrained to remark that I had indeed discovered "a brave stone."

Another stalker—he is now an old man and on the retired list—lived in the same wild glen, and many a story had he, too, to tell of the hills. Full of quaint sayings was this veteran. I remember how on one occasion he stated, while remarking on the weather which had been experienced during that season, how that "at times the sun would gain the masterpiece, but that then the wind would get up, and the mist would come down, and the atmosphere would become most ungenial." Talking of the expeditions of a certain ornithologist, he once remarked of the person in question that "at times fine weather would accompany him " —an expression which sounded with great charm when spoken by this old hillman in his own characteristic way.

In a lonely bothy, in the very heart of Scotland and of the hill country, there formerly lived an old watcher who had the true charm of the hillman, and whose fund of reminiscences, told in his own inimitable way, seemed incapable of being exhausted. Now this veteran has retired—the hill was getting too steep for him, he simply remarked—and the bothy is inhabited by one of a younger generation. His predecessor took an interest in the birds which had their homes on the hills near his solitary abode. On fine July days he would climb to the very highest tops, and would sit quietly watching the snow buntings entering and leaving their homes amongst the rough granite "scree," or, as he put it, "dancing on the hill in the sunlight."

In the bothy field mice live, and my old friend used to spend the evenings in taming his small companions. After a time the mice lost their fear of him, and even fed on crumbs which he placed on his boot, striking each other comically with their paws in their efforts to obtain as large a share as possible of the feast.

An experience which this old watcher had on one occasion was one which will bear setting down here. On a certain July afternoon, after a day of sun and oppressive heat, a heavy thunder-cloud gathered above the hill north of the bothy. The air had the stillness which often precedes a storm, and as the cloud lowered, twilight descended on that part of the glen, although the sun still shone with curious red light at the head of the pass. Without warning, instantaneously, a solid mass of water struck the hilltop opposite the bothy with a deafening crash. A surging torrent immediately rushed tumultuously down the hill face, leaving a deep scar—visible at the present day—and bearing in its course rocks of such size as to be beyond the power of man to lift. Almost at the same moment a second wall of water descended on the hill near the foot of which the bothy was built, the rush of water narrowly missing the small habitation and its solitary and shaken inmate. The storm soon passed, and the sun again shone out, but the debris washed down to the foot of the glen was so extensive that the river was held back, and a lochan temporarily formed there.

This veteran took his duty as watcher seriously, and a stray mountaineer was accosted politely, and interrogated as to whether he had "permission for the hill." The type of tourist which the old hillman despised was the one which imagined that the hills were free to all men. I remember well two individuals—a man and a woman—who were "spied" making for the summit of a hill up which no right-of-way existed. The old fellow started off in pursuit, but the climbers kept on their way at such a speed that he was forced to give up the chase. On his return to where I was sitting his quaint remark was, "They would not stop—they were a couple of dirty sparks." The

STALKING : EXAMINING THE HILL FOR A LIKELY STÀG.

STALKING: A DOUBTFUL GLANCE AT THE SKIES.

emphasis with which the last two words were spoken was sufficient guarantee of the contempt they conveyed.

The tourist on the hills is generally looked upon with suspicion and a tinge of contempt by the stalker. Once I noticed two forms in the distance. The stalker who was with me looked at them a moment through the glass, then put back his telescope into its case, uttering as he did so a single word, and full of meaning. "Towerists," he grunted, showing clearly that such unfortunate beings were utterly beneath his notice.

During the spring meeting of a certain Alpine club on the Cairngorms, the ascent of Cairn Toul (4,241 feet) was attempted during a wild day, with a northerly gale and heavy snow squalls. The mountaineers encountered Arctic conditions on the hill, and had to cut their way step by step up the precipitous face. Between the storms of snow they could be seen clinging like ants to the hill, and finally reached the summit in a blizzard so terrific that they could scarcely draw breath. The feat was regarded as an extremely noteworthy one, so that the stalker who, after hearing full details of the climb, mildly stated "that he could well believe it was rather *airish* on the top " seemed to those who heard him to have certainly put things in a way free from even the slightest suspicion of exaggeration.

At the fall of the year the hills surround themselves with a certain quietness and mystery. With the coming of darkness the roaring of many stags breaks the silence. So intent are they in throwing out their husky challenges that in the dusk it is possible to approach to within a couple of hundred yards of them. A fight in grim earnest between two stags is of rare occurrence. Encounters, half serious, half playful, are numerous; but no stalker with whom I have spoken has ever witnessed a battle to the death. A veteran keeper had, indeed, on one occasion come across a stag still warm, and bearing the marks of the antlers of his adversary where the fatal wound had been dealt.

The Land of the Hills and the Glens

Another stalker of my acquaintance once noted a stag lying apparently dead on the hillside after a fiercely contested struggle. A near view showed that the beast still lived, and through the hours of darkness this conquered warrior wandered painfully, slowly, away to the far hills, where the hoarse triumphal roaring of his rival echoed and re-echoed across the glen.

CHAPTER XII

AN LOCHAN UAINE

BURIED in the very heart of the high hills, so that no eye can see it from a distance, is the loch known in the language of the mountains as An Lochan Uaine—the Green Loch. The lochan has many brothers and sisters of the same name; but in its own case the designation would appear to be misapplied. Lying in a crater-shaped corrie facing full to the bitter north winds, the lochan is of so great a depth that the bottom cannot be made out, even on a day of strongest sunshine, and thus it would seem that the water should be known as An Dubh Lochan—the Black Loch.

Winter comes early to the lochan. In the low country the air is yet soft and mild when the first thin sheet of black ice makes its way slowly, quietly out into the dark waters. Many enemies are against it—this young ice. The springs which feed the loch still retain their summer heat, and fierce gusts of wind time and again restore the lochan its freedom. But sooner or later the waters are imprisoned, and the lochan sleeps under ice and, perhaps, heavy wreaths of snow, till the coming of another spring. Even the heart of the deep corrie which cherishes the lochan is over three thousand feet above the level of the distant sea, and at the head of the neighbouring Garbhchoire Mhor ("The Great Rough Corrie") is the home of snowfields which remain always unbroken from one year's end to another.

The eagle often sails above the lochan. On warm, sunny days he perches for hours on end on the hill-top above, enjoying to the full the light and warmth. In winter his form is dark against the snowy wastes, and

The Land of the Hills and the Glens

I have seen him speeding up the great glen against a blizzard of powdery snow so dense that it was almost impossible for me to look into the storm.

One summer's day a couple of eagles were hunting above the lochan. On every side ptarmigan swept across the hill in wild flight, anxious at all costs to escape their dreaded enemies. One of the fugitives was struck down by the leading eagle, and as it fell, his mate, following close behind, seized the small body and bore it off in her talons, perhaps to a ledge where a hungry eaglet awaited its meal.

The peregrine is rarely seen at the lochan, but on sunny days of June and July the wild and beautiful song of the snow bunting is carried down to the loch from the rocky "scree" above. During this season there is no night on the high hills, and this mountain songster may be heard in the intense stillness of the day-break when midnight is past but an hour.

To the lochan red deer rarely find their way. Food is scarce on the granite-strewn slopes, and the going is steep, even for a stag. Peace is in the glen always, for this part of the forest is a sanctuary, and no rifle breaks the stillness of the corrie or the great glen at any time. During the dark nights of October, maybe, when a southerly wind brings rain and mist low on the hills, the roaring of the stags in the glen below is wafted gently up to the lochan, or as the grip of the frost is loosened in spring and the snow becomes soft, an avalanche thunders from the cornice fringing the ridge above and piles up its *débris* on the ice-bound waters. The roaring of such an avalanche strikes on the ear like the muttering of distant thunder as the great blocks of snow and ice rush with ever-increasing speed and enormous bounds to Lochan Uaine.

Even during the long days of June it is late before the sun strikes on the dark waters of the lochan, for south-

68

The Sea Pool.

An Lochan Uaine.

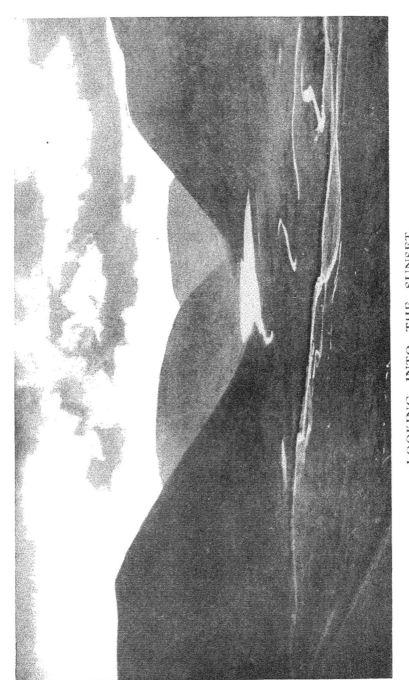

LOOKING INTO THE SUNSET.

Stron Bhuirich and Loch Bhrodainn.

ward the ground reaches an elevation of four thousand feet; and in winter, for months on end, the loch is in deep shadow.

The white mists hang low on the lochan for days together. Sweeping straight across from the distant Atlantic, the winds from the west often carry with them soft fleecy clouds which at first rest lightly on the hill-tops and gradually, imperceptibly, slip down to the surface of the loch, hiding it from the gaze of the eagle or of the soft-flying ptarmigan. I have often watched from the ridge above the playing of the winds on the waters of the lochan. No air current, except perhaps, from a due northerly point, strikes full on the loch. Often when a westerly wind approaching gale force was sweeping the mountain, I could see the eddying currents meeting on Lochan Uaine, and ruffling its waters from every point of the compass; white-tipped wavelets being hurried now in one direction, now in another, before the fitful gusts.

On quiet summer days, when the lochan lay unruffled by the faintest breeze, the veteran watcher of that part of the forest was wont, from the ridge above, to scan the waters of the lochan for the ripple of rising trout. But no ever-widening circle of wavelets rewarded his watching, for the infant burn which drains the loch descends in a series of cascades to the great glen beneath, so that no trout, however active, could force its way up. And then, one hot July day, it occurred to two fishermen that the loch might with advantage be peopled. With no difficulty they succeeded in luring fourteen trout from the big burn and placed them in a large biscuit tin. And now came the difficult part of the undertaking—the transporting of the future population up the precipitous hillside. The heat was intense, and the water in the tin had to be renewed with great frequency, for the fish rapidly exhausted the limited supply of oxygen and lay gasping feebly on their sides until a new draught of burn water gave them fresh life. At length the loch was gained and the trout, one by one, were liberated and sent forward into an unknown world. But one small troutlet, the baby of the pioneers, was not destined to explore the black depths of the lochan. All through the journey he had been pining and went out on to his last great journey just as the goal was reached.

I have often wondered what was the fate of these trout. Food they must have secured, for during the summer myriads of small insects play above the surface of the lochan, and the depths of the waters contain snails and other delicacies. The lochan, too, is of too great a depth for the ice to penetrate far beneath the surface, even during the most severe frost. One can only hope that the explorers are by now firmly established, and that the waters of the lochan, lonely from time immemorial, have at last been given small people to cherish in their gloomy recesses.

CHAPTER XIII

THE GLEN OF THE HERONS

AT the head of a sea loch, penetrating deep into the hills of the Island of Mull, is a narrow glen. Rising steeply from the loch the glen lies full to the south, so that it is in strong sunlight throughout the day, and on its heathery slopes grouse sun themselves and hill adders bask in the heat.

Running through the glen is a burn of clearest water, forming, as it hurries to the sea loch below, a chain of deep pools in which the water, quiet and limpid, shows as almost of a sea-green colour. In the months of spring many primroses bloom here, and wagtails glance, in long undulating flight, above the swiftly-flowing waters. From the mossy land at the foot of the glen comes often the trilling cry of the curlew, busy at her nesting, and amongst the black rocks in its upper reaches the dark form of the raven is sometimes seen as she enters and leaves her nest. Above even this, and where the burn has its birth, is the haunt of the hill ptarmigan and of the eagle.

Perhaps a mile from the sea the burn hurries through a narrow gorge, between steep rocks, and then falls sheer into a deep sun-bathed pool. Growing at the burn's edge a veteran oak here finds some little shelter from the winter's gales, but for all that is stunted in form—is not, I should say, twenty feet in height. But at the season of spring, to this tree there come a colony of wild-voiced herons, and the glen re-echoes with their cries.

To anyone conversant with the nesting habits of the heron in a country of woods this nesting site must appear strange indeed, for it is customary for this unwieldy bird to choose the very highest and most inaccessible tree. But here, on the Atlantic seaboard, no woods are present, so that the heron must content herself with a ledge on a rock, or the branches of a small and stunted tree.

And it is full early in the season that the heron builds her nest. It is, indeed, always a race between her and the raven as to who shall lay the first egg of the year. I do not think there is much to choose between them; anyhow it is a matter of a day or two at the most, and often the frost is very keen at this season, and the snow covers all the length of the glen. But it was on a day of soft winds and clear sunlight—the date was March 16—that I first saw the "Glen of the Herons" and visited their colony.

On the shores of the loch below many common gulls were mating, and their glad cries echoed among the rocks. Though the air had in it the breath of spring no growth was as yet showing amongst the hill grasses or the plants of bog myrtle, and the hillsides looked more brown and bare by reason of the strong sunlight upon them. As I made my way up the glen I could see before me many pairs of herons standing in ungainly positions on the branches of their tree, and as I approached they one by one took wing with harsh grating cries, and flew off to alight on some flat rocks near. Very curious did they look as they stood thus, outlined against the sky. But two of their colony were more reluctant to leave, rising indeed from their nests and eyeing me angrily, but not taking wing until I was almost under their tree.

These two birds had commenced to lay—in one nest there were two eggs, in the other but one—but the remainder of the nests were only in various stages of repair and construction. Some were almost finished and already lined with bracken, while others had nothing but the rough platform completed. In all there were eight nests on this small oak, and two more built on ledges of rock against which the tree had grown.

72

The Glen of the Herons

I do not think a better situation for observing the home life of the herons could possibly be imagined, for when standing on the heather above the waterfall I was actually above the tree, and could look down upon all the nests at a distance of not more than a dozen feet from them.

When freshly laid the eggs of the heron are things of considerable beauty. Of a pale sky-blue colour, and unspotted, they are in striking contrast to the bare brown branches of the tree and the hill grasses, bleached and browned by many a winter's storm.

On this day the mist was swirling past the higher reaches of the glen, and it was only occasionally that glimpses of the snow wreaths lying near the source of the burn, could be seen. This year the herons had eggs slightly earlier than the ravens that nested on the hillside opposite, for it was not until March 18, or rather later, that the latter birds produced their first hostage to fortune. By then, the mild weather had gone, and there was snow and frost on the hills, so that from the rocks above the raven's nest great icicles hung, and the nesting ledge was white with snow.

During another season, on March 21, two of the herons' nests each had three eggs, the remainder none as yet. This, I think, shows that in their time of nesting the birds are very punctual and do not depend on the weather to any great extent. That same year, on April 13, one of these nests had young which seemed about forty-eight hours old, the other still contained eggs.

By the 22nd of the month four of the nests had young, and the earliest comers were already developing into lusty young birds, which called incessantly in a very husky and feeble imitation of their parents' cry. During this day a companion and I fixed up a "hide" on the top of the rock in the hopes of obtaining some photographs of the parent herons at their nests. The weather was very fine and sunny, the snow-covered hills standing out in dazzling whiteness against the deep blue of the sky, while away to westward the sea breeze brought with it white-tipped wavelets from the Atlantic waters.

With much labour a hiding-tent was set up and the top covered with bracken, but although we waited for hours the herons could not summon up sufficient courage to face the strange erection, and we had to leave without success, nor did circumstances permit of our attempting any further photography that season.

That same year, on June 16—eight weeks later—my way took me past the Glen of the Herons. The glen was now clothed in its summer verdure. The primroses had gone, and belts of bracken grew luxuriantly. The old oak was now in full leaf, so that the nests of the herons were partially hidden, but the birds were still there, and on looking into the nests I was interested to see that one of those which held, in late March, three eggs, contained now, quite three months later, four eggs. Evidently these must have been a second laying, unless another pair of herons were tenanting the nest. Another interesting case was a nest which contained two small young on April 20 and which now held two newly-hatched young and one egg. Young herons remain long in the nest, and I doubt whether during these eight weeks the first brood could have been reared, the nest repaired, and a second clutch laid and hatched out. It seems more probable that some mischance befell the first family, and the parent bird laid a second clutch of eggs in the same nest.

In another season the Glen of the Herons was visited on July 7—a day when the mists hung low on the hills and when the south-west wind brought with it soft driving rain from off the Atlantic. On this occasion one nest contained two young, about a fortnight old, and, pressing close to them for their warmth, a tiny newly hatched chick. In another nest were two eggs and a new-hatched young one, while two other nests had large feathered young.

THE HERONS' GLEN.
Showing Six Nests in the Same Tree.

THE HERONS' TREE.
A Nearer View of the Nests.

The Glen of the Herons

The eyes of the young herons are of a singularly bright yellow colour, and their skin is of a curious hue, a sort of smoky blue. Thus the tree of the herons was still fully occupied more than sixteen weeks after the first eggs were laid—a protracted nesting season.

I do not think the herons use the burn of their own glen for their fishing, but along the banks of the sea loch they can be seen at every state of the tide as they stand motionless and expectant on the lookout for fish. Often, after dusk has fallen, I have been startled by the harsh alarm scream of the heron as, disturbed in his fishing, he has flitted past in the twilight like a restless spirit.

But it is not alone on fish that the heron feeds. In the spring, at the mating season of the frogs, he takes great toll of these clammy creatures and feasts also on their spawn : indeed, in late March every little knoll round the nesting tree is thick with half disintegrated masses of this substance.

The herons at times travel far to their fishing. From one heronry that I know at the north end of the Island of Mull the birds regularly cross the sea to the Island of Coll, more than six miles distant, where many lochans provide them with food in plenty. But the flight of the heron is a thing of labour should the wind be contrary, and I have seen one of these birds arriving not a little weary after his overseas flight, so that he was full glad to rest on the rocky shore of this rugged island lying to the westward of Mull.

Amongst the bird world the heron is a bird of evil omen. Nowhere is he left unmolested. The tribe of the plovers pursue him relentlessly, the sea swallows dart angrily at him when he blunders across their path ; all the gulls are his enemies. He has no friend at all, and yet it is hard to see why he should be held as an outcast, for he rarely attacks, and seems only too glad to escape notice, though unluckily for him he seldom succeeds in doing so. It may be that his somewhat uncanny appearance and stealthy habits are the reasons for this enmity towards him. Certainly the heron's life is rendered a burden to him whenever he strays from his nesting glen, and thus it is that he is only too content to alight quietly at his feeding grounds and, unseen and so undisturbed, to carry on his fishing.

CHAPTER XIV

THE QUEEN OF THE ISLANDS

WEST of the rocky headland that stands, dark and weather-beaten, between Loch Scridain and Loch nan Ceall, is a small rocky islet, Ernisgeir by name. During the season of their nesting, sea-birds in their thousands populate the island; at other times no living thing is met with here save perhaps a grey seal on passage to his breeding grounds, or a green cormorant resting awhile from his fishing. Even during days of summer calm when the Atlantic, to all appearances, is quiet as a loch, the swell breaks in white cascades on the island, and in the winter, with the passing of a south-westerly gale, the sea here is a grand sight as the great rollers cast themselves against the island, the spray enveloping even the highest parts of the rocks. Small and unpretentious as it is, and hidden away in obscurity, the islet is, nevertheless, known to the old people as "the Queen of the Islands," and the following tradition explains the origin of the name thus chosen.

It is said that the Lord of the Isles wishing the hand in marriage of the daughter of MacLean of Coll, the latter would consent only on the understanding that the Lord of the Isles should give his future wife as her dowry "Little Ernisgeir and all her islands," or, as the Gaelic puts it, "Ernisgeir bheag 's a'cuid eileanan." A small request seemingly, and one to which the suitor readily agreed. But when the marriage settlement came to be demanded, a claim was made for all the neighbouring islands, including the whole of Mull, since there were no small islands in the neighbourhood of Ernisgeir. Hence it

77

came about that to Ernisgeir was given the proud title, "Queen of the Islands."

In another version of the story it is said that the request was put forward by a nurse or foster mother (which latter class was common at that time in the Highlands) when she went to ask the Lord of the Isles for a patrimony for her child. To make the request small and likely to be granted without trouble, on being asked what land she wished, she replied that she would be quite satisfied with "little Ernisgeir and her islands," and the true meaning of the request was not realized at the time.

Even during recent years the appearance of Ernisgeir has changed. The old people of to-day remember the time when the grass grew long and green here, affording pasture sufficient for eight sheep throughout the year. Now scarce a blade of vegetation can be found from one corner of the island to another. It seems that the puffin, or, as he is called by the Highland fisherman, "Seumi ruadh," or "Red Jimmy," must be held responsible for this, since it was only at his coming, within the past twenty years, that all grass disappeared as the result of his burrowing.

But to the island, these companies of "herring birds," to give the puffin another local name, give a strangely cheerful look. I shall not forget the first time that I passed it close, crossing from Gometra to Iona in a motor-boat. While yet some distance from Ernisgeir the puffins in their hundreds flew out towards the boat, and accompanied it, without a cry—for these strange birds are almost always silent—well beyond the place of their nesting. This was a day of dull skies and—a thing rare in the Western Highlands—a steady downpour of rain unaccompanied by wind. On this day along the Gribun Rocks grey m'sts hung, heavy with their moisture. Of the hill-tops one could see nothing, but from out the mist cap there came many white waterfalls, for each hill burn was overflowing, and dried-up

The Queen of the Islands

watercourses were given a new lease of life as the flood water hurried seaward. Many solans, occupied in their fishing, passed and repassed Ernisgeir, for the herring is often plentiful here, and even if it should be absent the mackerel takes its place, and to the solan it is little inferior to the herring. It was not until evening that the wind came, a strong breeze from the west; but the rain still fell and the hills remained inscrutable beyond the soft barrier of the mists.

Another midsummer's day on which I visited the island brought with it "steady weather," as they say in the Highlands. A strong breeze from the east drew sharply down Loch Scridain, blowing through Glen More from the big hills. But an east wind of a morning is the sign of fair weather, and thus we set sail from the sandy shores of Iona with good heart. Our course took us past the disused quarries of the finest granite, and past green grassy islands above which sea swallows wheeled and skimmed gracefully. The ebb tide was strong against us, and after a time the wind dropped, so that the rowing of a heavy boat through waters still ruffled by a short sea, or "jabble," as the boatman termed it, was no light task. Even the sea air was warm this day, and at times the sun shone, though away eastward heavy clouds were gathering high above the hills as though betokening thunder.

It was after midday when Ernisgeir was reached and a landing made on its rocky shores. On this day the puffins had not come out to scrutinize the boat—I expect the noise of the motor had aroused their curiosity on the previous occasion—but as they saw that intruders were about to set foot on their nesting haunt they swarmed excitedly around them. With them, and wheeling and dipping gracefully on their long, slender wings, were numbers of Manx shearwaters, and on the sea there swam buoyantly a few plump black guillemots, handsome in their black plumage with that small conspicuous patch of white on either wing, and their red legs.

The Land of the Hills and the Glens

At the south end of the island the rocks rise precipitously, and here kittiwakes stood quietly on their nests or sailed on white wings above the sea. Curiously enough, the big cormorant is almost entirely absent from these Hebridean Islands, his place being filled by the green cormorant or shag, and of these latter there were many nesting on the day of this visit. Ungainly and seemingly plebeian birds are these green cormorants; still, they show great devotion and bravery when their eggs or young are in danger, and not infrequently refuse to leave the nest even when one is standing not more than a foot or two from it. At such times they will utter harsh and angry cries, and peck viciously with their strong bills. I remember once seeing a sailor hurl some heavy rocks at a shag guarding her brood, and although one actually hit the nest the brave bird refused to leave it.

As I left the island, the spring tide was at its lowest ebb, so that many rock pools, teeming with the life of the sea, were left exposed. Hermit crabs lurked in their depths, and numbers of sea anemones in brilliant hues awaited their prey, their many tentacles spread to the full.

Near to Ernisgeir, and hidden away beside that rocky promontory known as "Craig na h'Iolaire," or the Eagle's Rock, is a deep and gloomy cavern known as "MacKinnon's Cave." No ray of light penetrates its inner recesses, and the air here contains little oxygen, so that one feels oppressed in the cave and glad to emerge once more. On this day, setting our course for Loch nan Ceall, and sailing close in shore, its narrow entrance was passed near by.

Tradition has it that to this cave at certain seasons was wont to repair a Highlander, known as "MacKinnon of the Whelks," in order that he might there fast and humble himself. MacKinnon was a piper, and was in the habit of taking with him his pipes when he visited the cave. One day, when he was quite alone in the cavern, and playing a tune on his pipes, there gathered round him in the

The Queen of the Islands

intense darkness that prevails always in the cave, many evil spirits. Each time he would start playing the pipes, the spirits endeavoured to overpower him, but the pipes acting as a partial, though not complete, charm, they were for long unable to do this. In the language of the Highlander who gave me the story, "MacKinnon was then wishing that he had three hands; then he would have his two hands in the pipes, and the other in the claymore (or great sword) to cut down the evil spirits." The tune which he was said to have played on the pipes has been handed down, and can still be obtained.

MacKinnon was apparently overwhelmed at last, for the strains of the pipes slowly became more irregular and at length ceased—nor did the player ever emerge from the dark recesses of the cave.

CHAPTER XV

To the Isle of Mull the name "Muile nam Mor-Bheann," or "Mull of the Big Hills," has been given. In one of the songs of Duncan Livingstone, the Crogan bard—he who in the Gaelic was known as "Donnachadh nam Blar"—the island was thus designated, and now wheresoever the language of the Gael is spoken this song is known and sung.

But though Mull is guarded by many hills—the rough, precipitous slopes of Beinn Buie shielding the land from gales from the south, while rising from the Sound of Mull, Dun da Ghaoithe breaks the force of the northerly winds —there is one mountain that towers above the rest, so that for many miles to seaward it serves as a landmark, and even from the distant hills of Perth and Inverness can clearly be seen, and that is Ben More—"the Big Hill."

Compared with Ben Nevis, or the giants of the Cairngorm Range, Ben More is not high, for its summit reaches a level of no more than 3,163 feet; but whereas the bases of the Cairngorms lie more than fifteen hundred feet above sea level, Ben More rises straight from the waters of the Atlantic.

There is little heather growing on these hills of the far western coast, for the rainfall is extremely heavy and the soil is not suitable; granite, which heather loves, is absent, and the black basaltic rock does not favour its growth. Thus it is that Ben More, on its lower slopes, is clothed in rich grass, and nearer the top only a few stray mosses and mountain plants find lodging places amongst the sharp volcanic rocks.

Ben More Mull

At every season of the year Ben More has its own individual charm; but I think the hill is at its best on a sunny day of mid June, when all Nature is pulsating with life after a long and severe spring—and hereabouts the spring is late in setting its mark on the land—and when the air is of that wonderful clearness that one sees only when the summer is young. On one such day, early of the morning, I made my way through Glen More. The river was so low that scarce a trickle of water made its way seaward, but in a deep pool a large salmon lay waiting for the spate that would carry him to the upper reaches. Already the young of the dippers which frequent the burn had left the nest, but ring ouzels still tended their broods, and from the single telegraph line that traverses the glen, stonechats perched, scolding roundly as their nesting-ground was passed. No bird is more cunning than the stonechat in concealing the whereabouts of its nest, and I have had many patient vigils without discovering the site of the eggs or young. Standing perched on the stems of the fragrant bog myrtle, whinchats called anxiously. They too had their nests, but unlike the stonechats, which had thriving broods to care for, were still sitting on their eggs of pale unspotted blue.

When within half a mile of Loch Scridain, I turned from the road and made for the summit of Ben More, which stood, no more than three miles away, distinct in the clear sunlight. A few pairs of curlew tended their young on the lower slopes of the hill, but they were soon passed, and save for the occasional chirruping of a meadow pipit, or the "chack" of a wheatear, the hill was in silence. Away ahead one could see, outlined against the deep blue of the sky, many stags, and, on a different part of the hill and keeping separate from them, hinds and their young dappled calves were seeking out the cool breezes, or were sheltering behind rocks from the strong heat of the sun. On the rocks near the summit cairn an eagle sat awhile, digesting his meal, before sailing out on broad, motionless wings over the rocky corrie where a few ptarmigan have their home.

At length the shoulder of the hill was reached, from where I could see, spread before me, the sister lochs, Loch Scridain and Loch nan Ceall, reflecting the blue of the sky, and many islands on which the surf broke lazily. Here the ground was carpeted with plants of the cushion pink (*Silene acaulis*), and I was interested to note that the vertical limit of their growth was at least five hundred feet lower than on the more land-locked Cairngorm Hills.

Stretching away to Loch nan Ceall lay a broad grassy corrie well loved by the deer, and where buzzards circled and ravens croaked. From the shoulder to the cairn is a climb of some seven hundred feet over very rough boulder-scarred ground with only here and there a small grassy patch. Near one such patch I watched a cock ptarmigan, who ran up the hill ahead of me, and whose mate may have had her nest in the vicinity, but a careful search of that part of the hillside revealed nothing. The tracks of the deer were numerous here, and indeed led right across the summit of the hill, and I could see where stags had been lying, perhaps to catch the warmth of the evening sun as he sank towards the north-west horizon. In the shelter of the stones, plants of a certain mountain saxifrage—probably *Saxifraga nivalis*—were putting forth their buds, but no other flower grew here.

I think the summit of these far western hills must in fine summer weather have a temperature considerably lower than the Cairngorms. On the latter hills, after days of summer sunshine the great plateaux become so heated that the temperature is at times actually higher than in the glens beneath. Even on Ben Nevis I have known this to be the case. But with Ben More, and indeed all hills standing out into the Atlantic, the heat of the sun almost

Ben More Mull.

always draws in a cool breeze from the sea, which at a height of over three thousand feet is usually chilly even in the finest of weather.

I do not think the snow bunting nests on Ben More, though one summer's day I fancied I heard his song carrying up from a stony corrie lying north-west of the summit cairn. Indeed, bird life is very scarce on the hill—an odd grouse on the lower slopes and a few ptarmigan near the summit. No golden plover nest here, and on all the hills of Mull there are only a very few of these birds in the season of their nesting. Where the hill rises from Loch nan Ceall, numbers of curlew have their nests on a strip of boggy ground, but these birds do not ascend far, for the ground soon becomes dry and rock-strewn and unsuited to their habits.

I think Ben More Mull must be the most western hill of Scotland on which ptarmigan have their home. From what other hill in this country could one stand at a ptarmigan's nest and actually see the heavy Atlantic swell breaking almost at one's feet, with at times even the boom of the surf in one's ears as it breaks on the reefs by MacKinnon's Cave, away beyond the dark Gribun rocks?

A wild stretch of country lies before one from the summit cairn. Hill and loch and rocky island. Through the maze of hills this June day, the narrow Sound of Mull threaded its way, the blue of the reflecting sky, and on its sun-bathed waters the white sails of passing ships were vividly contrasted with the dark blue of the sea. Eastward, beyond the Firth of Lorne, lay the great hills of the mainland; Cruachan, with its twin peaks and, rising straight from Crianlarich, many miles distant, the conical hill known as Ben More, on which the snow lingers till well on in summer. Then, bearing north, the great range of the Glen Coe Hills, with Ben Nevis, their chief, still carrying big snowfields on its upper slopes. Lying well sheltered in its land-locked bay, the town of Oban showed mistily through a thin blue smoke of its own making, and near it could be seen the wide entrance to the long and winding sea loch—Loch Etive, which receives into its waters that famous salmon river the Awe, and, continuing even farther inland, penetrates into the very heart of the hills. Nearer, and set at the entrance to the Linnhe Loch, lay the green island of Lismore—its Gaelic name signifying the "great garden" because of the fertility of its soil—with its stout lighthouse built on the small island at its southern extremity.

From the summit of Ben More after sunset, if the night be fine, one can see the rays from many far-flung lighthouses shining across the great spaces of the Atlantic. Westward, Dubh Hirteach shows its bright light for thirty seconds; is eclipsed for ten seconds, with ten seconds of light after that, followed by ten seconds of darkness. Not far away, so it seems, is the great light of Skerryvore, showing a flash every twenty seconds. Bearing north, one sees the quickly flashing light of Scarinish on Tiree, and north of that again the small flashing light of the Cairns of Coll seems dim and feeble in comparison with the bright steady glare of Ardnamurchan a few miles from it. Northwest, Heiskeir light stabs the darkness with its sharp flashes, and even the rays of Barra Head Lighthouse, sixty miles to the westward, are clearly visible. Then again, turning southward, one sees the beacons showing the approaches to the Isles of the Sea, with their swift currents and their many jagged rocks, and away beyond that again, beyond the lonely Isle of Colonsay, the fixed light on Rudha Mhail, in Islay, shows as a warm beacon in the summer twilight. I have named only a few of the lights which are clear. I should think that at times even the light on Innistrahull, off the north Irish coast, would carry to Ben More, but I do not know that it has ever been identified.

Lying northward of the summit cairn of Ben More is a deep corrie, with sides of precipitous rocks, or treacher-

BEN MORE MULL.

OYSTER CATCHER'S NEST.

Ben More Mull and its Snow-beds in the Distance.

ous scree, so that a descent into it is a matter of considerable difficulty. Among the rocks the rose-root flowers, and clumps of parsley fern unfold their delicate fronds with the melting of the snow. The sea thrift grows here, flowering, however, considerably later than at its usual habitat at sea level, and saxifrages open their white flowers. In the corrie is fine grazing, so that deer are almost always here from June until the coming of the autumn snows, and ptarmigan croak quietly from the rocks. In the corrie snow lingers till late. On one occasion it was not until July 7 that the last trace disappeared, and for a hill so much under the influence of soft Atlantic winds this is a very late date. But the following year the snow had gone from the hill by mid-June, and at the time of the climb of which I write no remnant remained.

This June day, in the shelter of the summit cairn, the midges made themselves felt even at this great height, and each time I halted on the lower reaches of the hill during the descent they were exceedingly hungry.

When about one thousand feet above Loch Scridain, which lay almost directly below me—so steep was the descent—I found a small loch where was the nesting-ground of several pairs of common gulls. During the whole of the day I had watched the birds soaring gracefully at immense heights, evidently revelling in the joy of life which a day such as this must give to all nature, but as I approached their lochan they flew angrily towards me, uttering fierce cries. Several young birds of various ages crouched on the grass or endeavoured to escape by swimming, and I saw more than one nest containing eggs, which for some reason had been deserted.

Arriving at sea level, no breath of wind disturbed the loch. Gradually the flood tide crept inward, covering the sun-baked rocks and parched seaweeds with its cool waters. Along the shore sandpipers called anxiously, for their young were near them, and in the air was the scent of many yellow irises with which the shores of the loch are covered at this season of early summer.

Lying as it does well into the Atlantic, Ben More attracts to itself many clouds. When Iona and the Ross of Mull are flooded with summer sunlight, I have time after time seen dark storm-clouds hanging low on the hill, and heavy rain frequently falls here when in the glens below the day has been one of the finest. How often, when all the rest of the sky was of a deep blue, have I watched tiny clouds gathering on the hill and being carried on the arms of the breeze past the cairn. Often these infant clouds as they touched the hill would imperceptibly gather strength, so that soon the whole hill-top would be shrouded in thin filmy mist on which the sunlight played as it strove to dispel the vapours.

In the season of winter the great storms of rain which at that time visit the Hebridean Islands fall on Ben More in the form of snow, and it is then that the gloomy corries on the north-east side of the hill are filled with drifted snow hurried thither on the gusts of the south-westerly gale.

And when the mists lift a little, so that the hill-top is clear, the snow can be seen whirled in great clouds past the cairn in the arms of the storm.

One day of March, when much snow had quietly fallen on the hills overnight, without warning a gale from the west sprang up shortly after midday. On the summit of Ben More the air was bright and clear, but behind the hill lay banks of dark storm clouds. Across the hill-top thick blinding clouds of snow were being carried, and so great was the force of the wind that, instead of drifting into the corrie below, the snow, as it was swept over the narrow summit, was caught right up into the clouds, so that it could be seen trailing into the sky, outlined in the form of a long white cloud against the blackness of the storm behind it, and gradually merging into the hurrying mists.

Ben More Mull

Full often does the wind in the season of storms, sweeping down from Ben More, rush through the narrow Sound of Ulva, so that the spindrift boils on the surface of Loch Tuadh, and on Loch nan Ceall the waves run mountains high; when at the same time on the waters of the Firth of Lorne scarce a breath of wind stirs, and when Loch Buie is calm in the sunlight.

But gradually, with the strengthening power of the sun, and when the season of spring is already well established in the glens, the brown grasses of Ben More become tinged with green, and at last this verdure extends even to the summit of the hill, so that the dark rocks seem still more sombre on account of this touch of life that is about them. There are times when at the close of a summer's day, when the sun is sinking behind Ulva and when the whole of the hill is bathed in a warm soft light, that Ben More takes on a strangely soft and kindly aspect, but for all that the hill is essentially one of wild and rugged grandeur —in its element when the storm-clouds race in from the sea, and when the roar of the gale re-echoes from its gloomy rocks, where the eagle revels in the storm.

CHAPTER XVI

THE LOCHAN OF THE RED-THROATED DIVER

On a lochan, set high among the western hills and remote from the haunt of man, a pair of red-throated divers have their summer home.

During months of winter the lochan is held in the grip of the frost, and all the grasses of the boggy plateau are browned and scorched by the bitter winds from the north. But the divers have never seen their country thus, for it is not until the uncertain spring has given place to glorious days of June, when the sun is high in the heavens and all nature is glad to live, that they arrive at the lochan.

I recall to mind a June day, near midsummer, when, accompanied by a kindred nature lover, I made my way to the lochan. The coming of summer was backward that year—May had brought with it a succession of northerly winds, with no warmth in their breath, and the hills still held their covering of snow. Even with the coming of June the air remained chill, but to-day, the longest of the year, the morning breaks calm and mild. On the hills the mist lingers, hiding from view their higher corries, but with the strengthening of the sun the sky clears, and in the air is a warmth unknown for many a day.

From the veteran stalker's house at sea level, the path to the lochan rises abruptly, winding its way up a steep hillside facing full to the south. The hot sun draws out many delightful scents from the mountain vegetation. The perfume of the bog-myrtle's opening leaves, the scent of the youthful bracken fronds, of heather and young grasses, all lie on the still air and charm the senses. On the top of the hill, stags stand—their growing antlers outlined against the blue of the sky—finding some relief from the heat in the gentle sea breeze which is drawn in from westward. Opposite are dark cliffs where buzzard and raven have their home, and near by a pair of golden eagles rear their brood in an inaccessible precipice, rising sheer from the sea.

We reach the tableland, and see before us the lochan of the divers. From here a fine view lies stretched out to the westward. Below us the blue waters of a sea loch reflect, in their rippling, the sun's rays, and the Atlantic swell can be seen making its course shorewards with measured rhythm. Far out on the waters the Island of Colonsay lies half hidden in the haze, and beyond that the hills of Islay are dim and indistinct. On the plateau Nature is very still in the warmth of this summer day. We make our way to the lochan's edge. No sign of life reveals itself to us. The breeze ruffles the water's surface, and the water has that reddish hue denoting the presence of much peat.

The lochan holds, so it is said, trout of great size, which may at times be seen in the dusk of a summer's evening as they swim leisurely near the surface; but they rarely rise to the fly, and during to-day not one of their number shows himself. No sign of the red-throated diver is to be seen on the loch, but a search round its banks reveals her nest containing a solitary egg quite warm to the touch.

Weeks of dry weather have caused the loch to shrink, so that the diver must have difficulty in hoisting herself up on to her nest. There is the usual beaten track running from the nest to the water's edge, for the diver when leaving her egg invariably follows the same path. The nests of the diver tribe are placed always within a foot or, at the outside, eighteen inches, of the water's edge, for the birds when disturbed never take wing from the nest, but creeping to the water, dive noiselessly in and remain concealed till the passing of danger.

It was not till we had been in the neighbourhood of the lochan some little time that the diver showed herself, and evidently thinking concealment was no longer possible, rose from the water and flew round at great speed and at an ever increasing height, uttering grunting cries. Speeding away in the direction of the sea, she did not reappear for some time, but when she did so, "volplaned" at express speed and with great rushing of wings until she had almost reached the water's surface, when, her timidity overmastering her anxiety for her eggs, she sailed up once more and disappeared from view.

It was towards evening that we revisited the lochan. The air was very still. Clouds of midges danced in the sunlight, but no rising trout broke the lochan's quiet surface. Then, as we watched, from the shelter of an overhanging bank the diver swam out into the water. Swimming deeply submerged and causing scarcely a ripple as she moved, she reached the centre of the lochan and there remained quietly facing us. From where we watched, every detail was plainly visible, and the beautiful red plumage on her throat contrasted strikingly with the dark waters. I do not think that she actually saw us, and her suspicions were gradually quieted. Diving noiselessly, she re-emerged a few feet away from her nest and, now feeling confident she was unobserved, clambered up the bank and apparently dried her plumage awhile before settling down on to her egg.

As I write the days are now lengthening and the grasses on the tableland are once again pulsating with life. If all goes well with them the divers will soon reach their lochan from their winter home in the south.

During the long summer days the hen bird will set about choosing her nesting-ground, and constructing her rough nest. At the evening she will leave the lochan,

NEST OF THE RED-THROATED DIVER
On the Shores of a Hebridean Lochan.

NEST OF PEREGRINE ON A HEBRIDEAN ISLAND,

flying down to the sea below to her fishing, and even when brooding she will still visit the salt water for her food, where her curious call-note will often be heard at the hour following sunset. Then, when midsummer is past, and when the stags are losing the velvet on their horns, the young divers will be taken to the sea beneath, and the lochan, now in quietness and in solitude, will be left in undisputed possession of its great trout.

CHAPTER XVII

THE TRIBE OF THE SEA SWALLOWS

WHEN the air is again warm, and the south wind blows softly, the sea swallows reach the grassy islands of the Hebrides, where they will remain for the season of their nesting. They are about the last of the migrant tribes to reach us. The wheatear has long since come—her young are already hatched; the swallows have been with us for some weeks; even the swifts are screaming in restless flight round the ruined castle; and yet the sea swallows linger in their coming. Then one day of mid-May, when the sea thrift has begun to tinge the shores with pink, one sees the gleam of snow-white wings above the green waters of the quiet ocean, and realises that the sea swallow has once again reached the place of her nesting.

And what flight can rival in grace that of the sea swallow? True, there are birds with more power of the wing—take the keen-eyed solan, who presses on his way grimly, unswervingly, in the teeth of a gale the sea swallow would be scarce able to face; or the dark mountain eagle, sailing with steady wings against the force of the storm—but in daintiness and in the poetry of flight, the sea swallow is unique among birds.

The tribe of the sea swallows consists, so far as the British Isles are concerned, of five distinct species, namely: the roseate tern, the sandwich tern, the lesser tern, the Arctic tern, and the common tern. Of these the sandwich tern is considerably the largest, but both he and the roseate tern are found only in a few favoured localities, and it is the three latter species that people the wild islands and the unfrequented shores of the Hebrides.

The Tribe of the Sea Swallows

Between the common and Arctic terns only small differences exist, so much so that it is a matter of great difficulty to distinguish them on the wing. But I think there is a well-marked difference in the call-notes of these two birds which has not in the past been sufficiently emphasised. The cry of the common tern is, generally, two or three sharp notes, followed by a long-drawn and harsh scream. The call of the Arctic tern is not long-drawn, but a very sharp and piercing screech, oft-repeated while the intruder is in the neighbourhood of the nest. When the two species nest together, as is often the case, this difference in the call-notes should, I think, serve to distinguish them.

Then there is that small and active member of the tribe, the lesser tern, much less common than either of the above, but very charming in its habits, and confiding in its ways.

The tribe of the sea swallows are, with the petrels, the last birds to commence their domestic affairs, for they are dependent for their food on the multitude of small fry—sand eels and the like—which live in the surface waters of the sea, and until the strong sunshine has warmed these waters the fry do not make their appearance.

The longest day is past, and full summer come to the land of the hills and the lochs ere the sea swallows are in the midst of their nesting. But even with midsummer the air is not always warm, and the north-easter blows cold over the face of the waters. One such day I crossed the Sound of Gunna—that strip of tide-torn water lying between the islands of Tiree and Coll—and saw many of the sea swallows at their nesting. The sky was clear, this day of late June, but the north wind was strong and keen, so that the sound was wave-flecked, and the track of the tide, hurrying northward against the wind, could plainly be seen by reason of the heavy sea which it was raising. Many islands lie in the Sound of Gunna. Of all sizes are they, ranging from wide grassy slopes where highland cattle feed, to small bare rocks scarcely showing above the water at the top of a spring tide. On most of the smaller grassy islands Arctic terns were. nesting, and in passing, one could see them brooding on their nests or arriving with their catch of fish.

Periodically they would, on a sudden impulse, take wing together and fly swiftly out to sea, gliding low over the water's surface, and returning to their nests within the space of a minute or so. It would be interesting to learn the reason for these sudden excursions. Certainly the common gulls nesting near appreciated them, for they gave them the opportunity of purloining a few of the eggs before the terns could return and drive off the marauders.

Depending, as they do, entirely on the presence of the small fry on which they feed, the terns will either not nest at all, even in a well-known haunt, or will leave it before nesting is completed, should the fry be absent from the neighbouring waters. An interesting case is that of some grassy islands in the Sound of Mull. The terns were nesting here in their thousands in a certain year. The following season —a very cold summer, and with much northerly wind— not a single bird was to be seen. The year after this they had returned, though, I think, in reduced numbers, while in the fourth season the islands had their former dense population.

In this latter year the arrival of the terns seems to have been considerably later than usual. On May 14 and 15 great numbers of the birds were fishing in a bay a good deal to the south of these nesting-grounds, and it was not until May 23 that they were first seen at a well-known nesting-haunt where they usually arrive punctually on May 6. A small island on which they nest was found by the terns to be already occupied by a colony of black-headed gulls. A fierce battle commenced, continuing all that day and into the night, and recommencing early next morning. At length the terns withdrew, leaving the gulls in possession, but a few days later the sea swallows returned with reinforcements, and again engaged the gulls, ultimately driving them off and taking possession of the island.

In the Hebrides the terns do not nest much before July. On two successive seasons, during the last days of June, I passed a small island where every foot is tenanted by the terns during their nesting, and not more than half the number of birds had arrived. Returning later, about July 10, the island showed a white cloud of screaming birds moving restlessly above their nests, which almost all contained fresh-laid eggs.

In one Hebridean island the Arctic terns lay their eggs on a broad expanse of fine grazing ground, the grass being cropped short by sheep and cattle. Here the birds do not even scrape a slight hollow, but lay their eggs on the soft grass. They are very zealous of these eggs, and swoop viciously on any intruder, uttering short and piercing cries of rage. Near here is a bog where dunlin used to nest, but now the terns, and with them some black-headed gulls, have taken up their quarters here, and the dunlins have gone elsewhere.

At times the Arctic tern nests on a long shingly bay, near the pasture land, where the southerly swell breaks with a deep booming, and where many shells, some of them large and of great beauty, lie piled up at the mark of the high spring tides. Here, when the sky is clear, the terns leave the incubating of their eggs to the sun, and wheel and fish in graceful flight, straying far from their nests, but mysteriously appearing should danger threaten. I have often crossed the bay at the time of their nesting and never saw them actually leave their eggs unless the day was dull and cold. On one such day, late in June, I was surprised to see three whimbrel still lingering at the water's edge. As I approached they rose and headed north-west, repeatedly uttering their high twittering note, pitched in different keys. Could it be that they still intended nesting in the northern latitudes where they have their summer home, or were they non-breeding birds, meaning to stay hereabouts through the summer?

On this day I examined several terns' nests. In each case the eggs were laid on fine sand, and the nesting hollows were lined with small pieces of shell brought from another part of the shore. Near by there was nesting a solitary pair of lesser terns. Flying with short and sharp wing-beats and uttering her pleasing call, the hen left her eggs while I was yet some distance away. There were two eggs in her nesting hollow, but it was devoid of even a lining of shells, the eggs reposing on a layer of fine sand. It is not usual for one pair of lesser terns to nest by themselves; the birds generally breed in small colonies and have the ringed plover as their companion, from whose eggs, indeed, their own are sometimes difficult to distinguish.

All through August the tribe of the sea swallows are rearing their young. I have seen eggs as late as the middle of that month, and it is not until September that the birds set out on their southern migration. A Highland boatman—a keen observer—near whose home many terns nest, tells me how on a September day all the sea swallows from the island near his home congregate together. Then, rising to a great height and wheeling and screaming, they gather themselves into line and set out on their journey. But, strangely enough, it is not to the south, making towards Skerryvore and the Irish coast, that they set their course, but due north. Can it be that they make the passage round Cape Wrath and the north of Scotland and go south by way of the North Sea, or is their northerly flight a short one only, to join themselves, perhaps, with other colonies in the neighbourhood?

Even in October one sees terns fishing along the coast, and a Hebridean fisherman assured me that on one occasion he had seen a solitary individual as late as December.

Being such late nesters, the terns, when they set out for the south, leave behind them numbers of their young of

Lesser Tern about to Brood on her Newly Hatched Chick and Egg.

Lesser Tern and her Chick.

A KITTIWAKE WITH HER YOUNG.

all ages, the migrating instinct proving stronger than the parental one.

But I do not think their migration is a hurried one, like that of the birds which have difficulty in obtaining food on their journey; for the sea swallows appear to make their way leisurely along the coasts, feeding on the sand eels as they go, and gradually reaching those southerly regions where, with the sun shining warm and the sea blue and unruffled, they will pass the winter months till the call of summer once more brings them north to their well-loved nesting-grounds.

CHAPTER XVIII

RUDHA NA H'UAMHA

Away in the west of Mull there stands, guarding the shores of that island from the eager waves of the Atlantic, the Headland of the Caves, or, in the language of the Gael —"Rudha na h'uamba."

I think that of all districts of the island—sparsely populated and inaccessible as it is, even in its busiest parts— this is the very wildest. No crofter's dwelling can be found along the headland; indeed, the foot of man may not tread its rough slopes from one year's end to another. It is given over to the Atlantic, and to the winds which come thither from the vast regions of the sea.

The last outpost of civilisation is a tiny croft overlooking the blue waters of Loch Scridain, just where the loch gives place to the restless heave of the Atlantic, and here dwells a Gaelic speaking shepherd with his wife and family. Often have I visited their home at every season of the year—during summer sun and winter storm—and each time I have received a welcome of the best, one which could be given only by those who live their quiet lives close to the heart of Nature. The good wife of this croft is never idle. She has many things to occupy her time. Yet I have never known her too busy but what she was eager to give the traveller the best that her home could provide: scones and oatcakes hot from the girdle, things to refresh one greatly after a long tramp across the hills. Many pairs of stockings and socks does she knit during the dark winter nights, from the wool which she has herself spun and dyed. At this spinning and dyeing of the wool there is indeed none in the island to beat her. Of a summer's afternoon I have watched her drawing from the various hill plants the dyes which they hold; the yellow from the bog myrtle, or from the foxglove, the black from the young alder shoots or from the elder twigs, the green from the heather, the brown from the crotal—a stone-loving lichen—and have marvelled at her skill.

It is in early summer, in fine weather, that the Headland of the Caves gives a view of unsurpassed beauty to those who can penetrate thus far. One such day, when I lay on the hilltop above the headland, will linger long in the mind's eye.

In the morning heavy thunder-clouds hung low on the hills, and not the faintest breeze stirred the heather, but towards noon the sky brightened and the air was of a clearness I have never, I think, previously known.

From the croft my way lay up the heather-clad hillside. Above me buzzards soared, their plumage glinting in the sunlight, and ravens passed with husky croak. Beneath me lay Loch Scridain, its waters ruffled by the gentlest of sea breezes and, at its entrance, the sands of Iona lying white in the light of the sun. The hill-top is not high—it stands less than 1,500 feet above sea-level—yet I do not think that it has ever been my good fortune to be favoured with so extensive a view as during this day when summer was yet young, and the scent of hill plants was everywhere.

Westwards there lay, as it were at my feet, many islands set in the sun-flooded sea. Tiree, with its white sands shining, and almost joining it, rocky Coll. Then away beyond them stood the distant sentinel islands of Barra and South Uist. More to the south I saw clearly the granite-built lighthouse of Skerryvore—a needle-like object of white, set in the midst of a great waste of waters, and even beyond it, and near forty miles from me, I could make out, through the glass, herring drifters rising and falling on the swell, which, with the exception of a day or two in each year, is always present at the Skerryvore bank.

It was to the south that the view was most extensive. Jura, with its three conical hills, appeared almost in the foreground, so clear was the day. A little beyond, and farther west, stood Islay's hills, and then away beyond the Mull of Cantyre, and lying to the westward of that headland, lay, full seventy miles distant, mile upon mile of the Irish coast, with its many hills showing faintly on the horizon. The largest of these I took to be Slieve Snaght, above Lough Swilly, and I thought that I could identify Malin Head.

Every now and again, white fleecy clouds, floating gently in from the Atlantic, passed up Loch Scridain below me, but though their line of passage was considerably below the level of the hill-top, they did not come thus far, making, instead, for Glen More, above which thunder-clouds had gathered and were shedding their rain.

Northward there lay mile upon mile of the wildest mountain land, a country studded with lonely lochans reflecting in their depths the dark blue of the sky, and with the peace and stillness of the hill spirit brooding over all. No man passes here, maybe, throughout the season, and the land is given over to the buzzard, sailing on tireless wings through the day, and the timid mountain hare.

With what force must the mist-laden Atlantic gales cross this lonely country! I noticed that in certain places not one single plant was growing, though soil for them was indeed present, and that certain parts of the hill plateau had been swept and scoured till they were smooth and level as a still lochan. No grouse haunt these wind-swept places. No pipe of the golden plover breaks the stillness, no trill of the curlew falls on the ear. But the buzzard mews often here and the raven, too, is not always silent. Nor is the hillside quite forsaken by all bird life, for cheerful wheatears call sharply in resentment, and more dif-

Rudha na h'uamha

fident meadow pipits utter their plaintive alarm cry as the stranger crosses their nesting grounds.

Years may pass, yet they set not their mark here; world wars may rage, so that the best of the life's blood of a nation is spilled, and the earth may seem a saddened and altered place, yet the spirit of war would scarcely penetrate to this wild and mist-laden land, and silence always would reign here save for the rush of the gale, and the deep note of the waves as they break on the rocks far beneath.

Tradition has it that in this wild spot fairies dwelt of old. On one occasion a number of them went to assist a crofter living near, in weaving and preparing cloth. Having completed their task, they clamoured for more work. In order to rid himself of his too willing assistants, the crofter called out that their house was on fire. Immediately the fairies rushed out of the house in a body, nor did they ever return.

Even in the season of summer, mist often encircles the Headland of the Caves for days on end, when the green fields of Iona and the heathery wastes of the Ross of Mull are clear in the strong sunlight. On one such misty day, late in September, I visited the Headland. Scarce a breath of wind moved the surface of Loch Scridain as I pulled out from the quiet anchorage. The course was parallel to the shore and as near to it as safety would permit. Great boulders, worn smooth by the power of the Atlantic, were strewn along the sloping bank lying beneath the high cliffs, so that walking here was a thing of painful slowness, and it were better to use the sea as one's path. Where the shore was smoother, and little bays of shingle lay half hidden, there were strewn thickly at high-water mark many stems of laminarian seaweeds, cast up by the winter storms and now lying dried and shrivelled. Their value is nothing here, for there is none to gather them.

When within less than a mile of the Headland, the boat

was anchored in a narrow creek, out of reach of the swell, and the journey completed on foot. Lying strewn along the foot of the high cliffs are masses of basalt rock, encrusted often with pale blue crystals of great beauty. At one point also, there stands a perfect specimen of a fossil tree, embedded deep in the cliff, and still standing upright so that its shape and form may clearly be seen. Beyond it again is another such tree, in the same position in which it fell to the ground many thousands of years ago, and so near the water that with each tide it is washed by the waves.

Much wreckage is cast by the winter storms on these desolate shores. Drift wood in plenty lies amongst the rocks, yet there is none to benefit by it, so that it remains there from one year's end to another.

In former days the great sea eagle had her eyrie on the Headland of the Caves, and for her fishing was wont to sail out to far distant Tiree and its adjoining seas. Now the eagle has gone; indeed, there is scarce a single one of her species left in the whole of Scotland to-day, and so her lesser rivals the buzzard and peregrine hold undisputed sway in her old haunts.

As I left the Headland, a strong "breeze of wind," as the fisher-folk say, was drawing in from the Atlantic, and quickly the sea rose, so that the swell was booming on the reefs. Far out to sea the clouds came to an end and the pleasant Treshnish Isles stood out, the late September sun shining golden on them.

But at this season of the year the darkness falls all too quickly, and soon hill and sea were shut out in the gathering gloom, and all was silent save the restless surf as it broke with measured rhythm on the lonely rocks of the Headland of the Caves.

CHAPTER XIX

THE MAIL-BOAT

To the dwellers in the inaccessible Hebridean Isles of Coll and Tiree, the one link between themselves and civilisation is the small but sturdy steamer which, summer and winter, regularly brings to them their mails, and indeed, most of the necessaries of life.

Manned by a sturdy crew of Gaelic-speaking Highlanders, and in charge of a skipper who is one of the finest navigators of his time, the mail-boat succeeds in making her call at the narrow and rock-girt loch at Arinagour, in Coll, and at the surf-ridden Gott Bay, in Tiree, when no other vessel, either stranger or one "well acquaint" (as they say) with the coast, would attempt to make a landing.

I have many a time crossed over to the islands in the mail-boat, and each occasion I can clearly recall, but one which remains most vividly impressed on the memory was on a wild morning of early December. The previous day was dull and quiet, with mist hanging low on all the hills, and with the barometer extraordinarily low—it stood at 28.4 inches—and still falling. It was after dark when I started on my way to Tobermory, that little seaport at the northern entrance to the Sound of Mull, from which the steamer was wont to start out before daybreak. There was as yet no wind, but across the northern sky the aurora played incessantly. From the north-western horizon, where the sky was free from storm clouds, pale shafts of greenish light shot up, remained for a few seconds, then vanished, to reappear elsewhere. As far as the zenith the glow extended, and flickering shafts of light, as though from sheet-lightning, lit up the sky. Below, the dark waters of that narrow sea-way, the Sound of Mull, lay almost unruffled, with the flashing lights of the Grey Islands at Salen and Craignure showing up brightly in the clear air.

An hour or two after midnight the quietness was suddenly broken by a raging gale from the south, which tore up through the Sound of Mull with the speed of an express train, and heaped up the tide before it, so that it was by far the highest of the year and flooded many of the low-lying haughs. At the hour of the sailing of the mail-steamer the gale was at the height of its strength, and the darkness was so impenetrable, what with mist and driving squalls of rain, that the captain decided to await daybreak at his moorings.

So it was that shortly after eight of the morning the boat put out from the sheltered anchorage of Tobermory and set her course for Kilchoan, on Ardnamurchan—the first port of call. We had steamed perhaps a mile when a patch of open sky, green, and fringed with wild storm clouds, appeared to the west, followed a minute or two later by a terrific squall of rain and hail, which flattened the turbulent sea as though oil had been cast upon it. And with the deluge there came, as is customary on the western coast, a shifting of the wind from south to west—a wind which, while bringing with it the full force of the Atlantic swell, was more favourable to the chance of making a landing at the islands whither the ship was bound. As we came in sight of Kilchoan we could see the ferry-boat put to sea in the teeth of the gale and laboriously move forward, foot by foot, propelled by such powerful thrusts that the strong oars bent almost to the breaking point. But just as it appeared possible that the ferry would in time be able to fight her way out to the steamer the wind increased to hurricane force, with blinding hail and rain, so that one feared the small craft might founder—it was now quite hidden from view by the squall—and the mail-boat headed to sea for her life and set her course for the distant Isle of Tiree. And the wildness of this passage I shall not easily forget. Constantly swept by heavy seas—even on the bridge we were every moment drenched with spray—the plucky boat forged ahead surely and steadily. At times the sky would show patches of watery greenish blue, and even a feeble sun would occasionally light up the rocky outline of the Isle of Coll. But with the momentary ceasing of the rain the sea ran even yet higher, and, to add to the force of the gale, a strong spring tide was running dead against the storm. Once, as we passed by Loch nan Ceall, Ben More stood out for a moment, clad in unrelieved white and with driving mists swirling past its cone-shaped summit. Past the group of the Treshnish Isles, with the outlying members of the islands bearing the full strength of the Atlantic rollers, and we should have been well in sight of our destination; but the mist was so thick that no land could be made out, and now even the skipper—who knows these rock-strewn waters as very few can do—seemed not without anxiety.

After a while the mist lifted a little, and before us lay the turbulent waters of the creek known as Gott Bay, with its dangerous sunken rocks through which we must thread our way to the pier. Once into the bay the wind blew to us from the land, and as even a strong wind from this quarter is favourable to a landing, I expected to be able to be put ashore, the gale notwithstanding. But I had not realised the power of the wind.

Though our arrival had been watched by a small crowd in the shelter of the pier, and although the skipper brought his ship to within thirty yards and less of the pier itself, the gale was such that no one on the shore could stand on the exposed portion of the pier to throw out a rope, and we were obliged to steam out to sea once more, our object unaccomplished.

We now set our course for the Isle of Coll, and for this run we had a fair wind and sea, so that in spite of some very heavy rolling, I think we must have covered the distance in record time. Loch an Eatharna in Coll gives rather more shelter than the landing place on Tiree, and so it was possible to put ashore the mails and a few half-fainting passengers who moaned piteously and incessantly. I think that on this occasion the unfortunate passengers for Kilchoan were deserving of more than a little sympathy. They had joined the boat at Tobermory expecting to be set down at their journey's end after half an hour's sail through comparatively land-locked waters. As it was, they perforce endured at least eight hours of wildest Atlantic storm, and ultimately were set ashore at Kilchoan late in the afternoon in a state of collapse. As the captain quaintly observed, " They have indeed had their ninepence worth." (Ninepence being the fare from Tobermory to Kilchoan.)

Other memories are of still and frosty days of winter, days of setting out from the Island of Mull and looking back on to the snow-capped hills bathed in the rosy light of the dawn. Save for the slight heave of the Atlantic, the waters were glassy calm on these days. As we neared Loch an Eatharna in Coll one clear morning of mid-winter that I remember, the sun rose red and big from behind the summit of Ben More and flooded the island before us in its rays. One saw far afield these clear mornings, and the sea was wrapped in quietness and mystery those early hours before the coming of the sun.

And with the lengthening of the day, and the coming of the dry weather, one might see, when sailing the Passage of Tiree of a fine March morning, many heather fires burning on the hills of Mull—above Calgary, on Ulva's Isle, perhaps, or on Ben More itself, and again on the high country of Ardnamurchan. One great fire I remember seeing far away to the nor'ard. It was, I think, on Skye, and the whole of the horizon was blotted out in the blue smoke. And very good did the scent of the fires seem as it was wafted out on the sea. On one occasion, after a long spell of dry, frosty weather, some of the hill fires got the upper hand of those who kindled them, and burnt for several days, so that at night red beacons shone brightly seawards, and those on the outer islands wondered what they could mean. But these times of fine weather were of good cheer for the crofters, for on the low islands the frost is never severe, and thus they could go ahead with their ploughing or could burn their piles of tangles. Some of them, perhaps, would put out to sea in their skiffs, and would set their long lines for cod and ling and conger eels, lifting them just before the arrival of the mail-boat so that they might send their " takes " to the southern market.

And when spring had merged into summer and the days were long and fine the salmon nets would be put out along the shores of Mull, and the mail-boat, on her return run from the islands, would bear across toward Calliach Point and the fishermen would put out in their small boat with their catch of fine salmon straight from the sea. One day of early May the air was extraordinarily clear as we crossed to the fishers, and the snow-covered hills of Skye seemed but a few miles away, although in reality close on forty miles distant. This, I think, was the only occasion on which I have been able to see the sharp outline of Dunvegan Head, in the north of Skye, from these waters; and even behind that, and perhaps sixty miles off, was the conical point of one of the distant Applecross Hills, dazzling white against the deep blue of the sky.

On such fine days the crew of the mail-boat would be very busy, for after the frost and wet of the winter there would be much painting to be done, and the masts and woodwork would have to be scraped and revarnished. And as the crew worked industriously they would speak rapidly to each other in the Gaelic, and to the stranger from the south their tongue would seem curious.

During the war the mail-boat was taken away to do her share in the fighting. I often thought of her breasting the short, steep waves of the North Sea, with, maybe, a bleak and

The Land of the Hills and the Glens

desolate shore in view, and dodging here and there through mine-strewn waters, where in the end she met her doom.

And I think she must often have wished to feel the heave of the Atlantic and to see the sun rise from behind Ben More, or sink of a summer night behind the rocks of lonely Barra Head.

CHAPTER XX

SKERRYVORE

A GREY September morning, with the wind strong from the nor'-west. For days now the weather has been unsettled, and a heavy swell is breaking on the reefs that guard this small isolated rock from the waters of the Atlantic. The steamer which is to make the relief at the two storm-swept lighthouses of Skerryvore and Dubh Hirteach, lying not so many miles apart, but both of them far out at sea, lies at anchor in the Sound of Iona, rising and falling gently on the swell.

Thick drizzling rain is falling, and the day is long of breaking. It is still dusk as anchor is weighed, and the boat slips out through the sound, heading nor'-westward in the teeth of the wind, and making for the lighthouse built on the wild rock of Skerryvore (Sgeir Mhor, the Big Rock) twenty-five miles distant. Ahead, the sky is thick with mist and rain, and soon the view of the land is lost.

Nothing meets the eye save an expanse of storm-tossed waters. Sunken rocks—the Torrans—lie about us, and from time to time cascades of spray shoot up into the air, where the Atlantic swell meets the reefs. A wild part of the coast is this, and many a ship has found her doom on these rocks. Our vessel is powerfully built, as she must needs be in order to withstand the storms of winter, but the head-seas are slowing her down.

One sees many birds on these waters of solitude. Solan geese fly past, making their way hither and thither in search of fish. The flight of the solan is a thing of immense power, so that even the gulls themselves seem puny and feeble in comparison; but then the solan is essentially a being of the sea, and rarely indeed does he fly over even the narrowest strip of land. Farther out from the shore, fulmar petrels cross the bows, their flight strong and free, and excelling that of the gulls. Seldom is it that they move their wings, speeding and glancing with soaring flight above the waves, their wings held out stiffly, more, perhaps, resembling the wings of an aeroplane than those of a bird. And they fly in silence always.

Ahead, on the port bow, a trawler is seen labouring heavily. And now ahead the grey form of the lighthouse is showing, and one can see the spray being hurled high above the rocks. Making its way with swallow-like flight against the wind, and following the dip of the waves for shelter, a storm petrel crosses the bow, and nearer to the rock solans are fishing.

It is well on to low spring tide as the anchor is dropped a few hundred yards from the lighthouse, and already a chain of rocks, running out from the main rock to the southward, are beginning to show themselves, and to break the force of the swell at this anchorage. A tern is fishing in the comparatively sheltered waters here, and a rock pipit is resting awhile on migration, while the head of a grey seal swimming close in to the rocks is seen.

There is only one small creek where a landing is possible to-day, and a red flag, displayed from the rock, notifies the steamer where that landing is. Even with a strong boat, and a crew knowing the waters thoroughly, it is not easy to reach the landing place, or, once there, to maintain position, for the surf is breaking in and threatens to throw the boat up on to the rocks.

On landing, it is learnt that the keepers have experienced a wild night, with a very heavy tide on the rock, and one can see pieces of tangle lying at the foot of the tower, showing that the tide must have submerged the whole rock. The foundations of the tower are of solid granite, the door being placed, perhaps, twenty feet above the ground, with a set of copper steps leading up to it. From the top of the tower the roaring of the waves and the rushing of the gale is heard, and a wild view lies beneath.

The relief is soon accomplished, and we return to the steamer, weighing anchor immediately and setting a course for the lighthouse on Dubh Hirteach.

One cannot but realise how lonely a life it is that the lightkeepers lead, but there are many things of interest to be noted if one is a lover of Nature, as the men so often are. In the course of conversation I learned how on one occasion a grey seal was seen to land on the rocks with its captive, a good-sized cod. Although its victim was not yet dead, the seal commenced methodically to skin the fish, holding it firmly and ripping it up with its flappers, afterwards tearing out the backbone. On another occasion a seal was seen under water with a large cod, which it had disabled but not killed. The seal was playing with its victim in much the same way as a cat does with a mouse, releasing the cod, and having watched it for a while swimming feebly, pouncing on and seizing it again. My informant also told me that only a few days before the relief he noticed a solan goose come to the surface of the water holding a fish across his bill. He was in the act of shifting the position of his prize in order to swallow it, when a black-backed gull swooped down, snatched away the fish, and swallowed it before the surprised solan had time to remonstrate.*

On the passage to Dubh Hirteach the wind and sea are with the boat, and she travels fast. Moving southwards on migration, companies of great shearwaters pass by. In their build and flight they resemble their lesser relative the Manx shearwater, skimming and gliding on their powerful wings just above the crests of the waves, and constantly "banking" to obtain the full advantage of the

* *Note.*—Solans almost invariably swallow their catch *before* emerging on the surface after a dive.

wind. As Dubh Hirteach is neared, a heavy surf is seen breaking on the reef lying to the west of the rock on which the lighthouse is built, the spray driving like smoke before the strong wind; and on the rock itself a heavy swell is breaking.

It is not possible to-day to make a landing direct on to the rock, but the strong motor launch is lowered, and in her the lightkeeper and a small supply of provisions are carried to within a few yards of the rock, and are hoisted on to the latter by means of a derrick. While the relief is being effected, members of the crew are busy fishing over the rails of the steamer, and succeed in landing some good mackerel and saithe. Small birds are flying around, or are sitting lightly on the disturbed surface of the sea, uttering subdued, twittering cries. Their flight reminds one of the phalarope, and they ride on the water with the buoyant grace of these birds, sitting erect with their shapely necks held well above the water's surface. Through the glass one can see that there is much white about their necks, so they are probably not of the red-necked phalarope species. It may be that they are grey phalaropes on their southern migration, but the rough sea makes observation difficult. I hear that a couple of dunlin are annual visitors to this lonely rock, arriving at the conclusion of the nesting season, and leaving about the end of October. For a number of years they have been welcome visitors, and go by the names of "Tommy" and "Johnny." So fearless are they that they will come when called, and will feed almost out of the hand.

The relief effected, the boat heads northwards, and an hour's passage brings us back to the Sound of Iona, where the steamer is anchored and we are ferried ashore in smooth water.

CHAPTER XXI

LOCH NAN CEALL

OVERSHADOWED by wild hills, round which the mist-laden Atlantic wind weaves many clouds, lies a quiet sea loch.

It is rare that any craft darkens its surface.

Months may elapse between the visits of the small cargo steamer which brings to the crofters their meal and flour from the south, and apart from an occasional yacht in summer time, the loch is deserted, save for the skiffs of the lobster fishers, which put to sea early of a morning from Gribun shore, or from the quiet Sound of Ulva.

South'ard, the hills rise steeply to a height of more than three thousand feet, with dark precipices around which the silent-flying raven croaks, and green corries where the stags feed of a summer evening.

Many burns rush swiftly from the corries of the big hills to the loch. But even after days of torrential rain, when they roar in full flood, the waters retain their crystal clearness, for their source is on the stony plateaux and their course traverses rocky ground the whole length from parent spring to estuary.

To the east there lies the mainland, with all the hill country of Argyll spread out before the eye, and north the desolate Isle of Ulva, and that wild headland of Treshnish, where the Atlantic waves break in rushing spray when the wind blows strong from the south-west. Westward of the loch lies the Atlantic, and away on the horizon the Isle of Tiree. But it is only on a clear day that one's vision carries thus far, and then the houses seem to stand straight up from out of the water, so flat is this distant island.

The Land of the Hills and the Glens

I know the loch at all seasons of the year—in winter, when for days the roar of the gale echoes through the cliffs, and in summer, when day succeeds day, with no cloud showing in the sky, and when the waters of the loch are of a pale transparent green, so that the forests of great seaweeds may clearly be seen many feet below the surface, and amongst them big conger eels stealthily gliding.

It is, I think, during the darkest months of winter that one sees the loch in its grandest mood—months, when for days wild storms of rain and wind surge in from the sea and the waters are a turmoil of white breakers. At length, perhaps, the wind veers a little—from south-west, maybe, to north of west, at once dispelling the low-driving mist clouds and showing out to sea a sky of steely blue with grey hail squalls and dark thunder-clouds on the horizon, and with the drifting snow swirling across the tops of the higher hills. As the squall approaches the loch at great speed—for the gale continues unabated—vivid lightning comes from the storm cloud, and above the rush of the wind the thunder crashes and rolls among the corries of the hills.

At one point along the southern shore of the loch the rocks come sheer to the water's edge, and a precarious passage is made for the narrow road that traverses the island. During nights so dark that even the sea beneath was invisible, I have made the journey along the loch side, and have found the wind so strong that it was difficult even to stand against it. The roar of the surf beneath, the roar of the wind among the rocks above, the thick driving mist strong with the scent of the sea—on such nights as this one felt the spirit of the storm brooding darkly over the loch. There are many days of December when the force of the wind is such that the waters of the loch are caught up in whirlwinds and carried hither and thither; when the gale, eddying around the cliffs, rushes in gusts of hurricane force, now from the west, now from the east, with in between these gusts, a lull, uncanny in its stillness. I have seen, on such days, cormorants attempt to raise themselves from the loch's surface, and have seen them beaten down to the water by the storm so that they gave up the attempt at flight.

There is always a certain risk in using the road beneath the rocks on a wild night of wind and rain, especially after frost, for big rocks often break loose from the cliff, and bound in great leaps to the road below. It was many years ago that a tragedy was enacted at the small dwelling which used to stand at the foot of the cliff. One wild night a great rock, many tons in weight, breaking loose from the hill above, crashed into the house, in which a newly married couple had just established themselves. The house entirely disappeared, and no trace was ever found of its inmates.

How different do the cliffs appear in early June when the air is still and warm and when the rocks are tinged with pink blossoms of many plants of *Silene acaulis!*

During clear days of early spring, when the wind still carries with it a nip of frost, but when the sun shines warm and bright, buzzards sail across these rocks, and the raven may be seen carrying sticks to her nest. On the summit of the cliff the peregrine stands for hours motionless, scanning the country round him, or wheels in strong flight across the sunlit waters of the loch.

Concerning the name of the loch much conjecture has arisen. On the maps one will find the spelling "Loch na Keal," but in the Gaelic alphabet the letter "K" does not exist. The most probable derivation is, I think, "Loch nan Ceall," or the "Loch of the Burying Grounds," for on its shores are several such places, the most famous being on the Island of Inchkenneth. A derivation of some interest I had from a veteran Highlander who was no mean scholar and could write the Gaelic well—a somewhat rare accomplishment among the past generation. His opinion was that the name was "Loch nan Ceall," or "The Loch of the Round Gravelly Bluffs." This word is not known to the present generation of Gaelic speakers, but certainly near the head of the loch the hills are scarred with gravel, one especially, which in the clear midsummer light shows up red and prominent from many miles out to sea, and is noticeable even from Tiree and Coll.

Guarding the entrance to the loch are the two islands of Inchkenneth and Eorsa. Lying well out into the loch, Eorsa breaks the force of the west wind, and gives good anchorage for a ship in the wildest gale from that quarter. The island is uninhabited, save by the sea birds which have their home here. In winter, woodcock frequent the long heather, while in summer its shores are peopled by colonies of terns.

On Inchkenneth is the burying ground of many Highland chiefs. One farm stands on the island, and often during winter weather the farmer is cut off from the mainland for days and even weeks on end; for no boat can make the passage of the Sound when the great squalls sweep across from Ben More.

As the days lengthen, and the snowy corries of Ben More become streaked with black, many oyster catchers people the shores of the loch. Certain of these birds are always present, even in the dead of winter, but these winter visitors take their departure northwards at the coming of spring and are replaced by oyster catchers who have their winter homes to the south'ard. "Gille Bridghe," as the oyster catcher is known in the Gaelic, is quite fearless during the season of her nesting. I have counted over a dozen pairs of these birds brooding their eggs within a few yards of the road that runs by the loch.

It is said that the name "Gille Bridghe," or "Saint Bridget's Lad," was given in olden times to the oyster catcher because when the saint came first from Ireland to convert the Long Island (the name by which the Outer

L^och nan Ceall

Hebrides are known) to Christianity, she had with her an oyster catcher in each pocket, and on her arrival turned them loose.

Where the rocks are lying piled one upon another, the shelduck has her nest, so hidden away that only the expert may locate it, and on the boggy hillsides, a few hundred feet above the loch, many curlew have their homes.

In these days of May, when the south wind blows gently, and when the air is once more warm, it is good to visit the loch, for now a new bird note falls pleasantly on the ear—the cry of the whimbrel or lesser curlew. It is only on the journey to their northern nesting grounds that the birds linger at the banks of the loch. By the end of May the last of them has passed on.

With the coming of the fine weather the tribe of the herring enter the loch, and following them as their lawful victims there enter also many bird people, so that the waters are animated and cheerful. On many evenings of June I have sailed into Loch nan Ceall from the Atlantic, and these visits will linger long in the memory. The sun sets late among these western islands and after nine o'clock (G.M.T.) of an evening still shines soft and rosy on the unruffled waters, for by now the last of the breeze has died away and the loch is entirely quiet.

As one slowly makes one's way up to the anchorage at the head of the loch, puffins and guillemots cross one's path, and circling high overhead on untiring wings solan geese scan the still water for fish. On Ben More the setting sun throws its rays, lighting up those green corries and dark rocks on which the winter snowbeds still linger. These were days when the weather for weeks at a time was of the best, when day succeeded day on the loch and always the sun shone brilliantly, when the land wind blew strong from the east of a morning but veered westward with the turn of the day, so that the sea breeze ruffled the loch's surface of an afternoon.

The Land of the Hills and the Glens

On one occasion, in midsummer, I spent the night on Loch nan Ceall. The moon was near the full at the time, and as I made my way to the loch shortly before midnight the waters shone golden in its light. The land was in silence, save for the occasional cry of an oyster catcher, or the harsh grating notes of a corncrake from the young fields of growing oats. Ben More stood out dark against the star-studded sky. Its last snow wreath had dwindled under the strength of the midsummer sun until it covered only a yard or two of the hillside, and in a few days the hill would once again be clear of snow.

It was an hour after midnight when anchor was weighed, and a course set for the mouth of the loch. Already the north-eastern sky was showing a dull red glow, and the light of the moon was waning. From the dark rocks of Inchkenneth there came a deep booming note, as the tireless surf of the ocean spent itself among the hollow caves. And now the light was stronger, and the Treshnish Islands stood mirrored in the silent depths of the sea, and green-topped Staffa sought the first gleams of the rising sun. Now the waters were busy with many birds at their fishing, and companies of guillemots could be seen winging their way only an inch or two above the sea to their nesting grounds on the islands.

On a flat-topped rock many green cormorants stood, eagerly greeting the coming of the sun. Black guillemots too entered or left their nesting holes in the rocks bordering the loch, and on the many grassy islands the tribe of the sea swallows wheeled and dipped. On the flat rocks many brown seals were lying, and with them were their young, for the loch always shelters many of the seal tribe, and here they find good fishing and quietness. But their larger brethren the grey seals rarely enter the loch, for they prefer the wild outlying islands, and to feel the heave of the Atlantic.

As the mouth of the loch was gained the early sun shone

Loch nan Ceall

red through the morning mist on the quiet waters of Loch Tuadh—that northern sister of Loch nan Ceall, and joined to it by narrow Ulva Sound—while away to the nor'ard stood the black cliffs of Treshnish and of Calliach Point.

Gradually the summer gives place to autumn on the loch.

The wind blows chill from the north, driving the shoals of mackerel to the deeper waters, and sending the herring to sea, so that no longer are the solans sweeping over the loch, and the puffins bethink themselves of their journey south, while the last of the cormorants have left their nests. New bird visitors now arrive—the wary greenshank, with wild melancholy cry, and the great northern diver, of imposing mien, while one morning, after north wind, large flocks of widgeon may be seen riding buoyantly on the rough waters.

At night, great companies of geese fly overhead, as they make for their winter quarters on Islay and along the Irish coast, and in late autumn wild swans may sometimes be seen.

So that the loch is never deserted of living things, and gives food in plenty and shelter to many birds until with the call of the spring these winter visitors again set their course for the north, and their places are taken by those birds which at the approach of winter move southward to warmer, though not more hospitable, lands.

CHAPTER XXII

THE FIGHTING OF THE BLACKCOCK

THERE are few male birds amongst all the feathered tribes who do not, at the season of spring, give battle with their fellows for the favour of the demure lady who stands quietly by. But of all, I venture to think, the blackcock heads the list, for during the months of spring and early summer he fights each morning with great regularity. His battles are waged not only in the spring of the year, but during the season of summer and autumn as well.

In the Island of Mull—that island of wild hills and glens —there are birch woods clustering on the wind-swept hillsides, and it is here that I have many times watched, early of a morning, the blackcock, or "coilleach dubh," engaged in his favourite pursuit of fighting.

The birds are very conservative in their choice of battle-grounds, and return every morning to the same strip of hillside.

One such fighting place that I know is situated just above a remote sea loch, through whose narrow entrance the flood tide rushes faster than a boat can pull. Birches clothe the hillside, with here and there gaps in their ranks, where the hill grass is cropped short by the sheep and deer.

It is to one such open space that there come, flying noiselessly through the gloom as the first dawn shows in the eastern sky, the whole tribe of the blackcock of that neighbourhood. An enthusiastic keeper friend of mine erected, before the season of the battles had commenced, a couple of excellent shelters overlooking this ground, and one morning towards the end of April I made my way in

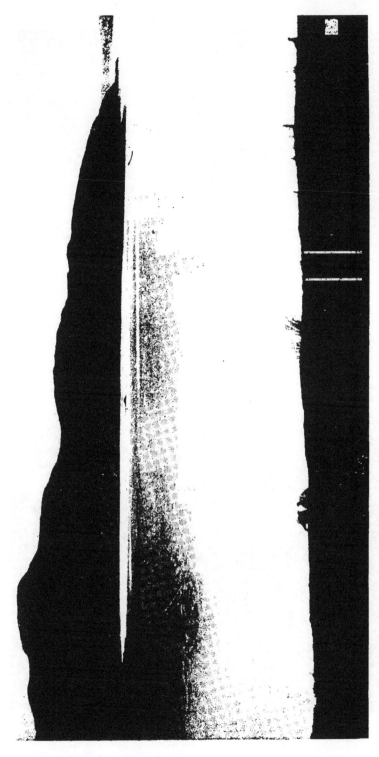

BLACKCOCK FIGHTING AT DAYBREAK ON THE SHORE OF A HEBRIDEAN SEA LOCH.

THE BIRTHPLACE OF A HILL BURN.

the twilight of the dawn along the shores of the sea loch to where I hoped to secure some photographs of fighting blackcock. At this hour, in the spring of the year, it is good to be abroad in the wild places. From a little grove a blackbird was striking up his flute-like song. The cheery whistle of oyster catchers and the cry of curlew fell pleasantly on the ear, and far up the hillside a missel thrush was tuning up his notes.

Arriving at the fighting ground, the keeper was awaiting me, and together we crept up the bed of a burn and succeeded in reaching the "hide" without alarming the fighters, which, as we could hear, had already arrived. Peering cautiously over the top of the hide, I could see many birds fighting hard only a few yards distant. Their curious bubbling note never for one moment ceased, and every now and again, as two individuals struck at each other with their feet, they uttered a sharp hissing sound, reminding one somewhat of the crow of a cock partridge. I think that the more one watches blackcock at their fighting the more one must come to the conclusion that much of this is somewhat half-hearted, and appears to be indulged in mainly with the idea of putting in the time and relieving the birds of their high spirits of an early morning. Of course, combats in earnest do take place and continue until one of the combatants is either killed or else put to flight.

On the morning of which I write many of the birds spent most of the time in confronting one another, in pairs, in crouching attitudes and with tails spread fanwise, from time to time leaping half-heartedly at each other but never having a real "scrap."

At length the sun rose, a ball of fire in the eastern sky. His reflection showed clear in the still waters, and the battle-ground of the blackcock stood out distinctly, with the grass encrusted with rime. With the coming of the sun the ardour of the blackcock abated and their thoughts turned from fighting to feeding, so that "sparring" was broken off, and the birds commenced to feed quietly side by side with their erstwhile antagonists.

Another much frequented battlefield of the blackcock is on the south shore of the Sound of Mull. Here, too, the spot chosen is on the outskirts of a birch wood, on a strip of comparatively bare ground. The main road runs only a few yards from this ground, and often, very early of a morning, I have disturbed the birds at their contests. More than once I have passed within a few yards of the fighting birds in a motor-car without even causing them to lift their heads. Having got past them I have stopped to watch their battles, with their soft, bubbling notes in my ears, and with the keen wind from off the Sound sighing through the birches and rustling the withered fronds of the bracken.

Though it is undoubtedly the mating impulse that prompts the birds to fight, it is rarely that the greyhens in any numbers frequent the battlefield. One often sees an odd bird there, or even two or three, but personally I do not think I have ever seen so many as even half a dozen watching the fighting of perhaps twenty cocks.

The blackcock is polygamous, but he takes no interest whatever in the eggs or broods of his several wives. I think there are, all the same, considerably more blackcocks than greyhens in existence, so that the former must frequently be perforce content with a single mate, if indeed, they are always able to procure even one.

CHAPTER XXIII

THE TRIBE OF THE WILD SWANS

I.—THE BEWICK SWAN

WHEN October has departed, and Polar winds, sweeping across Scotland from the north, tell of the approach of frost and snow, the gentle and graceful Bewick swan arrives at its winter quarters with us.

A certain island there is, lying out into the Atlantic, which every winter gives food and shelter to these travellers, and where no hand is lifted against them, so that they have little fear of man, allowing him to approach nearly, and being reluctant to take wing even when disturbed.

It was on a calm and clear day in November that I had my first sight of the swans. For some days winds from the north had prevailed, bringing snow squalls to the land, and piling up the drifts on the mainland hills. But on the island the snow did not lie, for the waters of the Atlantic had not as yet given up their summer heat, and the grass was still green. In the centre of the island a narrow creek runs inland from the south'ard. It is only at high spring tides that the salt water enters far—at other times a slow-running burn, with motion scarce perceptible, makes its way seawards. Up the creek were a number of Bewick swans, both young and old, the parents and their three or four youngsters in some cases still keeping together in small parties. In places the strips of water had been frozen across, and a few of the swans were asleep on the ice, allowing of a near approach before walking painfully over the slippery surface to the nearest lane of open water. At length they considered that I had approached too closely, and rose quickly into the air—and this is a point which distinguishes the wild from the domesticated swan, namely, that the wild species shows greater speed by far in launching itself into space than does our own mute swan, or even the wild duck.

The swans moved rapidly through the air by means of powerful wing beats, and passed backwards and forwards several times above the surface of the creek before slanting earthwards, and descending on the ice, their momentum sending them sliding forward a considerable distance.

A few miles to the westward lies a shallow loch, the home of countless wild fowl during the winter months, and here a few hours later I witnessed one of the most interesting and beautiful pictures of bird life that it has ever been my good fortune to enjoy.

The loch was frozen over, and at one end numbers of disconsolate gulls were standing on the ice. But at the far corner a great company of Bewick swans were swimming restlessly backwards and forwards across a narrow lane of open water, a lane which they had kept open by continued movement all through the night. A clamour of many notes was borne to the ear, notes musical and bell-like, and pitched in many keys. From time to time the sounds died away, but for a second or two only. A horse and trap passed along the water's edge, yet the swans paid little or no heed to it, so intent were they on preventing the frost from gripping the narrow waterway, and their voices carried far in the quiet air. It is always with their music that the wild swans herald the approach of frost; throughout the night, when the ice is silently binding the lochs, their notes are loud and insistent, never ceasing as they swim actively through the water, but with the coming of the thaw they are again silent, or nearly so.

Not often is the air so clear in the Western Isles as was the case this quiet November day. From the loch where the swans have their winter home a great expanse of sea and sky was to be seen. Eastward, across the waters, the hills held much snow in their corries, and the sinking sun tinged these snows with pink.

A country of silence, with the spirit of peace brooding over it.

On this low-lying island the frost is rarely intense. The next day a south-easterly wind brought with it an increase of temperature, and the narrow lane of open water on the swans' loch was rapidly enlarged, so that by night the whole loch was free. With the coming of the thaw, silence, or comparative silence, reigned in the swan world.

Through the months of December and January the swans frequented the loch. During the opening days of February—days when gale after gale from the west swept over the island, and fierce squalls of sleet and rain were driven before the wind—they were still there. But shortly after the middle of the month the wind dropped, the sea was again calm, and though the mountains lying to the east still retained their snow caps, the Bewick swans left the island, and at the end of the month the loch and creek were silent and uninhabited.

Of all the winter migrants to these coasts, I think the wild swans are the first to respond to the earliest breath of spring, but that year they left their winter quarters even sooner than usual. It is believed on the island where they are found throughout the winter that the swans know instinctively when the Baltic is open, and flight north directly this is the case. Whether this is indeed so, or whether the birds make the northward journey in short stages, it would seem strange that they depart a good two months before the white-fronted geese, for the two birds nest not far from each other in the far north, where snow still lies deep on the ground even during the early days of June. It is interesting to note, however, that the swans do occasionally return to the island after apparently having left for the north. Also that in the autumn they fly in from a northerly direction, while on their return in spring they come from the east.

There was one swan, however, that was unable to make the northward flight with his fellows that spring, and during the early days of March he lingered on the island, the sole representative of his race. He may have been suffering from a gunshot wound, for although protected on this island, the swans are often shot at on other islands to the north and north-west. Outwardly he had no apparent injury, and showed a remarkable degree of confidence. I first spied him from the top of a little knoll, from where a wide expanse of the island lies open to the view. He was asleep at the edge of a pool of water thinly encrusted with ice, and still slept, head buried deep in his snow-white feathers, as I reached him. Some movement of mine awakened him, but he showed little surprise or alarm, though when first he saw me he called once in that deep musical note so pleasant to the ear. He allowed himself even to be stroked, and it was only after several minutes' scrutiny that he decided to move, and walked sedately to another pool.

I have wondered what was the fate of this solitary and lonely swan, whether he recovered sufficiently to follow his tribe in their northward migration to the frozen tundras that approach the Pole, or whether he remained, an unwilling prisoner in a land that held no further attractions now that spring had come again.

In imagination, I can see him rising up into the still night air, and with deep honking cries rapidly winging his way to the northern plains, for surely he has gone in the spirit to that land of mystery which gave him birth, even if in the flesh he lacked the strength to make the great journey thither.

Bewick Swans at their Winter Quarters.

A Solitary Bewick Swan

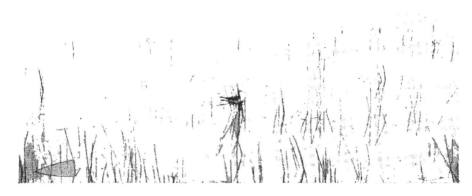

Red-necked Phalarope at its Summer Quarters in July.

Red-necked Phalarope—Throwing a Dainty Ripple as it Swims.

The Tribe of the Wild Swans

2.—THE WHOOPER SWAN

THE whooper swan does not, in ordinary circumstances, congregate in large companies as does his smaller cousin, the Bewick swan. Generally whoopers may be seen in twos or threes, swimming majestically on the dark waters of some mountain loch or eagerly feeding on the weeds, after the manner of the domesticated mute swan. And indeed they may not easily be distinguished from the latter bird, for in size they closely approach it. But whereas the mute swan holds his neck in a graceful arch, the whooper carries his outstretched, and after the fashion of a goose. Then again, there is this difference between the two birds, namely that the pronounced knob or "berry" at the base of the bill of the domesticated swan is entirely absent in the case of the whooper. These differences are important, for our own mute swan often migrates to a certain extent in a semi-wild state, and it is probable that a number of the reports which one reads from time to time of wild swans taking up their quarters on some loch refer in reality to mute swans in their wanderings.

It is late in the autumn ere the whooper swans make their appearance on the lochs of the Western Highlands. Nesting as they do, to a large extent, in Iceland, the winter's cold comes to them somewhat later than to those birds breeding well within the Arctic Circle, and so they are longer in commencing their migration south.

After a spell of north wind, in the early days of December, several whoopers made their appearance on a hill loch of western Ross-shire. It was on a perfect winter's day that I got my first sight of the birds. Not a breath of wind stirred on the moors, and the winter's sun, though low in the sky, was shining bright and warm on the desolate countryside. Climbing a small hill, I had before me a vast panorama of mountain and island. Northward

The Land of the Hills and the Glens

lay the rugged peaks of Caithness and Sutherland, and nearer at hand, and standing more to the eastward, was the great bulk of An Teallach, on which ptarmigan nest, and the eagle and raven have their home. Almost at my feet lay Gruinard Bay with a heavy surf from the north breaking on its sandy shores, and here a fleet of herring drifters were busy with the setting of their nets. Just showing above the nearer hills I could make out some of the hills of Skye, with the flat top of MacLeod's Table, rising from Dunvegan, prominent among them.

Beneath me lay a hill loch on which, their white plumage catching the rays of the sun, were seven swans. One lot of them, three in number, were standing in dozing attitudes, while near the edge of the loch the remainder were feeding on some water weed, propelling themselves powerfully through the water with heads well below the surface and pausing to emerge only for short intervals to draw breath. Careful stalking enabled me to approach the birds to within two hundred yards when, becoming uneasy, and apprehending danger, they one by one rose from the water with much paddling of feet, and on their strong wings made their way to the far end of the loch, a couple of miles distant. The next morning—the moon was near the full at the time—an hour before dawn I visited, together with a companion, the "loch of the swans."

In the western sky the moon shone clear as we set out, lighting up the dark waters of the sea loch which lay a mile or so to the westward. The ground was held fast in the grip of an intense frost, so that our footsteps re-sounded from its iron-bound surface, and the murmuring of a hill burn running through the glen was borne up to us on the still air. On the higher ground lay a powdering of snow, showing the well-marked tracks of fox and mountain hare, and of grouse which Reynard may perhaps have been stalking. Before the first rays of the December dawn had lighted the south-eastern sky we reached the loch, and there, near the outlet where the burn has its source, were the swans.

The company had been reinforced since we last saw them, and among them were two young birds. Although all the swans appeared to be dozing, they gradually changed their positions. Shining full on them, the moon lit up their snowy plumage, seeming to impart to it a tinge of warmth in which an artist's eye would have delighted. And indeed, are not the wild swans things of mysterious beauty in that they are, according to old Highland traditions, often none other than kings' children under enchantment? Have they not been seen on wild and lonely lochs, where they considered themselves secure from human gaze, to put away their plumage and assume human shape in their unsuccessful efforts to free themselves from the spells under which they have been cast?

As we watched them from the shelter of a great boulder, the light of the breaking day contended with the beams of the moon, and tints of red appeared among the clouds crossing the hill away to the south-east of us. All around us grouse awakened, crowing lustily as they left their beds of rime-flecked heather. A mallard, flying up the loch and emerging suddenly from the dusk, settled in the water, beside us, swimming carelessly around, and quacking excitedly as though challenging any possible rival in the neighbourhood; but his suspicions being aroused, he flew off again as suddenly as he had arrived. With the coming of daylight the swans roused themselves, frequently rising up in the water and vigorously flapping their wings. Soon they commenced to feed on the grass and weeds preserved from the frost beneath the water's surface, swimming quite close to us without suspicion as they breakfasted. The two immature birds, conspicuous from their fellows by reason of their plumage of brownish grey colour, fed by themselves for the most part. Until full daylight we watched the family party, and endeavoured to leave our hiding-place without arousing their suspicions. But in this we were unsuccessful, for the swans became alarmed and took to flight, the two youngsters being the last to move.

For a few days only the whooper swans remained on the loch. I imagine that their way led them south, for I know of no loch on the West Highlands where whoopers remain throughout the whole of the winter. It seems, indeed, as though many of the birds visit Scotland on their migrations only, and spend the winter to the southward of us.

But a few days later, when a north-easter cut through the heather, bringing with it bitter cold and squalls of driving snow, a fresh company of whooper swans, two old and one young, arrived on the loch. It seemed as though they were the parent birds still shepherding their full-grown offspring, for all fed closely together, heeding not the great cold, which numbed me as I watched them. So rough was the Minch this day that even where I sat the salt spray sped overhead, and the long-tailed ducks and other birds which frequented Gruinard Bay were driven to seek elsewhere for their food.

And on the wings of this storm the whoopers sped silently from us, so that with its passing the loch was left to the mallard which sit and sun themselves here, and the bald coots which call querulously to each other across the peaty water.

CHAPTER XXIV

THE PTARMIGAN OF THE WAVES

A STILL sea loch, with encircling hills, and a burn with waters of crystal clearness hurrying from the upper glens.

At its mouth the burn widens, and enters the salt waters by many channels intersected by shingly stretches. It is here that, with the first coming of spring, while the birches on the hillsides are still leafless, and when the song of the missel thrush is the only bird music to be heard, there arrive at least two pairs of ringed plover.

I have always thought that emanating from this unobtrusive wader was some quality of unusual charm, so that its Gaelic name, "Tarmachan na Teinne," or "the Ptarmigan of the Waves," seems to be a term of singular beauty, and well adapted too. "The ptarmigan of the waves" have, maybe, already paired before arriving at the nesting haunt; and it is pleasant to watch them, during sunny days of March, when the breath of spring is stirring amongst Nature's children. The lady on these occasions stands demurely by while the cock bird rises excitedly from the sun-warmed shingle and with curious, erratic flight—a flight that is almost bat-like—twists and tumbles, calling the while with soft and plaintive note. All the time, his wings move with scarce half their usual speed, and this characteristic of the love song of the waders—though I have not seen it set down in any book—is well marked also in the oyster catcher and the golden plover, to mention only two at random.

His love-flight ended, the bird, perhaps, goes through a display for the benefit of his mate, spreading out his tail fanwise, and otherwise making himself as attractive as possible for his lady wife to look upon.

The Land of the Hills and the Glens

It is not until the last days of April that the ringed plover commence their nesting. Little enough of a nest do they make, for after the manner of all the family of the plovers they content themselves with a slight hollow scraped out in the shingle, or amongst the sand dunes on which the sun shines with a blinding glare during days of summer heat. And, as plovers, they adhere to the habit that there should always be a number of "cocks' nests," as they are called, in the vicinity of the real nest. It may be that these are the doings of the male bird during his display, or they may be made by the hen in choosing the most favourable site. Be that as it may, they are almost always present.

One early May day the sun shone from a sky of deep blue, and though there was still a nip in the sea breeze, the waters of the ocean reflected the blue of the sky, and only the smallest of wavelets broke, glinting in the sun, upon the long beach of silvery sand that is the haunt of "the ptarmigan of the waves." As I sat amongst the sand dunes there came, from far out to sea, a company of bird travellers, making for the island. As they neared me, I heard that musical, twittering cry which is the call note of the whimbrel. Wintering far to the southward of our most southern shores, the whimbrel appear along the whole of the western coast during the first days of May with such regularity that they have earned for themselves the name of "May birds." In the Gaelic they are known as "Guilbinneach."

Swinging in, then, from the sea the travellers alighted upon the sun-baked ground close beside where I sat, and spread themselves out, searching with their long, curved bills for worms and such-like tit-bits. Near where they were feeding I came across a ringed plover's nest with two newly-laid eggs. In this case, although incubation had not yet commenced, the owner of the nest showed no little anxiety, running round me, and frequently uttering her soft, plaintive cry. In this instance the nest had no

134

The Ptarmigan of the Waves

lining of any sort; but I have, at times, seen nests charmingly decorated with shells of many colours, so that they stood out conspicuously against the sand.

Although I say it almost regretfully—so much is there, one might say, of charm of character in "the ptarmigan of the waves"—I think that, of all shore-living birds, the ringed plover must be one of the most careless—or can it be, most foolish?—in the selection of a nesting site. In support of this, I cannot do better than to give here an account of a season's nesting of a pair of these birds.

They arrived early in February at their summer home, but it was not until the middle of May that the nesting-ground was chosen. This was a strip of green grass, just above the level of the shingle, and by the bank of a deep pool of the burn. The nest, such as it was, was scraped out, and three eggs laid. At the approach of an intruder, the hen bird used to slip quietly off her nest, creep under the fence and cross the burn unobserved, but at times she might be heard calling nervously from the shingle on the far side of the stream. The nest was perilously near the reach of the spring tides, and on one or two occasions had narrow escapes. But one Sunday morning at the very end of May there came a heavy rainstorm out of the southwest. Mist hid the hills, and blinding squalls of rain swept the glen. Soon the burn commenced to rise rapidly until it was swirling seawards with swollen, turbid waters.

The moon was at the full at the time, so that the tides were at their highest, and to-day, carried forward by the south-westerly gale, the Atlantic waters filled the sea loch far more rapidly than usual. So it came about that, an hour before high tide, the nesting-ground of the "ptarmigan of the waves" was inches deep in water, and on the sea receding once more, the eggs were gone. Shortly after high tide I visited the nesting-ground—too late, unfortunately, to save the eggs—and found the ringed plover flying round her nesting-site with pathetic anxiety, seemingly uncertain as to what evil fate had befallen her unborn family.

But the birds were not long in recovering from the sorrow at their loss, for within a fortnight a new nesting site had been chosen and four eggs laid. This time the nest was on some shingle about five hundred yards from the burn, and just beside the ruins of a boathouse. Unfortunately for the birds, the neap tides were on when the hen laid her eggs. During the neap tides high water is several feet lower than during the spring tides, and this the birds found out to their cost a little later on. From the situation of the nest I could see that the eggs stood a very good chance of being washed away by the first high tide, so, together with a fellow bird-lover, kept the nest under observation during the evening high tides. In the Hebrides the evening high tide is noticeably higher than the morning, so it was from the former that the greater danger was to be expected.

As, day after day, the tides increased, we watched anxiously the waters creep nearer and nearer to the simple home of "the ptarmigan of the waves." One afternoon the tide approached to within a few inches of the eggs, and we made sure that, next night, the nest would be flooded out. I was away from home that day, but my companion reached the nesting-ground well before high water, and when the sea commenced to trickle into the nest, removed the eggs and laid them out of harm's way. The day was fine and sunny, and during the hour that they were out of the nest no harm befell the eggs, for the sun kept them warm until the tide again receded, the nest was left dry once more, and the eggs replaced. Both the ringed plover stood quietly near the nest when it was flooded, but curiously enough showed no signs of anxiety, and did not even utter their alarm cry. When the eggs were replaced, the hen returned to the nest as though nothing unusual had happened.

The Ptarmigan of the Waves

Next morning at six o'clock I visited the nest, but the morning's tide did not reach it. That day we were obliged to travel to the far end of the island, more than thirty miles distant, and there was no one to watch over the nest. A strong wind swept in the waters of the flood tide, and I felt sure that the eggs must be carried away. It was just at high water that I returned, and at once made my way to the sea loch, with the faint hope that I might be in time to save the eggs. But to my disappointment I found several inches of water covering the nesting site, and to make matters worse a strong wind was blowing off the land. Had it not been for this I believe I could have saved the eggs, as they would have been floating near, and their immersion would, in all probability, have done them no harm.

This time the birds seemed to realise their loss, calling repeatedly and moving restlessly across the shingle near where their home had been, and I felt sad for them, that their second attempt at rearing a brood should have ended in disaster.

More than those of almost any bird the eggs of the ringed plover harmonise with their surroundings, and so it is almost impossible to discover the nest by straightforward searching. By far the simplest method is to sit or lie quietly in the neighbourhood of where, by her behaviour, a ringed plover has given one reason for thinking she has a nest. And really this small wader, though apparently timid, is, in reality, quite confiding. Provided that the observer remains motionless, not many minutes elapse before she begins to run, in short hurried rushes, towards her nest. As she approaches her eggs she becomes more wary, and halts more often, or, perhaps, runs on at a tangent so as to mislead the enemy; but it is not long before, if one is the possessor of a good glass, one has the satisfaction of seeing her slip quietly on to her eggs, and settle down to brood them.

The Land of the Hills and the Glens

I have seen eggs of the ringed plover as late as the first days of August, and July nests are quite of ordinary occurrence, so that of all the plover tribe "the ptarmigan of the waves " is the latest nester.

Even when first hatched, the young chicks can run actively about, and they harmonise so closely with their surroundings that, when they crouch at the alarm call of their parents they are almost impossible to locate. It is then that the old birds show signs of very great alarm and often make believe that they are injured, trailing along just ahead of the disturber of their peace, and perhaps waving a wing helplessly in the air, or lying motionless, as though dead, in their efforts to decoy him from the vicinity of the young.

With the coming of autumn, "the ptarmigan of the waves " leave their nesting ground and make their way to the south, their places being taken by birds of their species which have nested to the northward of these islands.

Often of a dark autumn's night, when the wind sighed and moaned, and when the rush of the sea was borne to the ear, I have heard the plaintive cry of "the ptarmigan of the waves " from out of the pitchy darkness, and from the hearing of it have been transported in the spirit to sunlit islands where, beside a calm sea, I have so often watched the birds engrossed in the cares of their nesting.

CHAPTER XXV

THE ROSS OF MULL

AWAY to the west of Ben More, and hidden from the main-
land by this and sister hills, a long and narrow strip of
bog and moorland stretches out into the Atlantic. Some
twelve miles in length, it is given over almost entirely to
sheep, with a few crofts scattered along the margin of Loch
Scridain, and to a lesser extent on its southern shores which
are open to the Atlantic.

To the lover of the wild in Nature the Ross must always
have a charm peculiar to itself, for its beauties are many,
and are apparent at every season of the year. Its southern
seaboard is exceptionally wild and grand. For miles the
cliffs rise sheer from the sea, reaching a height of well over
a thousand feet, and the coast is quite uninhabited except
for the wild goats which have their home there. Towards
the western extremity this coast becomes less precipitous,
and here there nestles the little crofting community of
Ulsgean, near to long white beaches of fine sand, the
most remote of them bearing the Gaelic name of "Traigh
Gheal." Bearing still west, the island of Erraid—immortal-
ised in Stevenson's "Kidnapped "—is reached, and the Sound
of Iona, which acts as the western boundary of the Ross.

Away to the south of Erraid lie the Torran Rocks,
avoided by all mariners who have not a thorough knowledge
of the coast, and stretching far out to sea. Even on a fine
summer day the Atlantic swell breaks white on these rocks.
Some of them are only a few feet above high water mark;
others show only at low water, and on a still day of winter,
when the surface of the sea is calm but when a heavy swell
rolls in from the south-west, the waves shoot in smoke-like

spray against these dark grim rocks, to fall in glistening cascades all around.

On fine summer evenings, when the sun sets late behind the rocky island of Coll to the north-west, many herring drifters may be seen steering past the Ross as they make for the Skerryvore banks. Rising and falling on the gentle Atlantic heave, these drifters reach their fishing grounds by sunset, and lie to their nets during the short hours of twilight, lifting them again before sunrise and making their way to Oban, or to Mallaig, maybe, with their silvery catch. In the still air the smoke of the fleet lies on the horizon in the form of a dark cloud, extending for many miles on either side of the busy community. When a stillness has fallen over the waters many birds make their way to the herring fleet; indeed a dead calm is in the Gaelic known as "the Calm of Birds," from the fact that to the unruffled part of the sea where herring or any other surface-swimming fish are to be found, many birds wing their way, because there is no wind to obscure their vision. Here the sulair or solan dives with unerring precision; here also there come the grace-ful-flying shearwater, the guillemot and the wise razorbill, while the consequential puffin usually accompanies them.

And when full summer is come to the Ross of Mull big lythe—pollack as they are known in the south—arrive at the rocky shores from the deep waters of the ocean, and of an evening the fishermen from Carsaig and from Uisgean put to sea in their small boats, and, rowing over the ground where flourish the great seaweeds known as "Tangles," lure many of these strong bronze-coloured fish by means of the white fly, or the rubber eel. At such times no breath of wind ruffles the sea and away in the north-west sky the sun is dipping behind the horizon, and the rowers speak rapidly and incessantly in the Gaelic as they recall old anecdotes of these fishing-grounds.

I have noticed that the lythe seem to come in gradually from the deep waters of the Atlantic. Thus around Tiree they are plentiful even before the end of June. Then slowly making their way east, they appear along the Ross of Mull in July, and it is not until the latter end of this month that they penetrate to the land-locked waters of the Sound of Mull from where the ocean is invisible, and on either side tower great hills.

It is in June and July that the crofters look for the best weather of the season. In July the bell heather is in full bloom, so that its perfume carries far over the sun-baked earth. During this month, too, there come the hosts of that biting fly known as "the cleg," or in the Gaelic, "Greith leag," which with stealthy flight alights upon man and beast and sucks their blood. It is rare that these flies travel far out to sea, though in days of great heat I have known them accompany me throughout a two-mile row. In August the cleg is less in evidence, which is accounted for by the quaint belief that whereas in July he possesses both his eyes, in August he loses one of them, and cannot so accurately see his victims. Amongst the bogs there grows the St. John's wort, known in the Gaelic as "Achlusan Challum-Cille," a plant of magic power when found unexpectedly.

Throughout its southern coast line much wreckage is washed ashore along the Ross of Mull. From the summit of Beinn an Aonidh I have looked, of a July day, along its shores, and as far as the eye could reach have seen the drift wood piled up at high-water mark. The great cliffs prevent this wreckage being removed by land, and no houses are near enough to allow of boats being rowed hither. These wild cliffs are the haunt of the raven, the buzzard and the peregrine throughout the year. How different in their flight are these three birds. The buzzard and raven are strong, but leisurely fliers. They prefer to secure their food by stealth rather than by dashing flight. The peregrine is full of vitality—of the joy of life and the poetry of swift flight. From his perch on the topmost pinnacle of the precipice, the peregrine, on guard over his nesting-ground, sails into the still air with harsh screams. Mounting rapidly, he soon reaches the grey mist clouds that lie a little above the hill-top, and his outline becomes faint as he penetrates the vapours. Then swooping earthward at terrific speed, and with wings tightly closed, he seems as though he must plunge into the quiet waters of the ocean many hundreds of feet beneath him, until opening his clear-cut wings he shoots upwards without effort.

Most anxious of fathers is the tiercel, and he continues to utter his alarm cry till all chance of danger to his young has passed. But almost before the young of the peregrine have left the egg, the young ravens have taken their first flight, for is not the raven held to be the first of all nesting birds? An old Gaelic saying has it: "Nead mu Bhrighid, ugh mu Inid, Eun mu Chàisg, Mur bidh sin aig an fhitheach, Bithidh am bàs." Or, "Nest at Candlemas, egg at Shrovetide, bird at Easter; if the raven have not these he has worse —that is, death."

Of all birds the raven was—and is perhaps still—held by the Gael to possess the greatest knowledge. "Fios ceann fithich"—("the knowledge of the raven's head")—is a Gaelic proverb, yet these birds often choose for their nesting-site an easily accessible rock, where the nest can be harried or the young birds killed, while all around are great cliffs where they would be safe from the interference of irate keepers or shepherds.

There is something very attractive in watching on a fine summer day a family of ravens sailing across the rock-strewn moor in leisurely flight. Every now and again the parent birds tumble in the air with that peculiar movement so characteristic of them, and from time to time their deep croak carries through the quiet air.

On the grassy islands which fringe the Ross near its western end, red-breasted mergansers make their nests when full summer is come and the grass is long on the islands. Here the duck lays her large clutch of eggs, sometimes reaching a dozen or more, and leads forth her young brood to the waters of the Atlantic in mid-July. Here also are many of the gull tribe: the herring gull, of sinister aspect; the lesser black-backed gull; and on a few of the Torrans, the great black-backed gull himself. Of all British gulls he is the largest and most powerful on the wing. His cry is a deep, far-carrying note, less strident and more musical than those of his lesser relations, and he is always full of anxiety when his nesting-grounds are visited.

On the southern shores of the Ross, the solan is not often seen, but in summer time these birds of powerful flight enter Loch Scridain in large numbers. No prettier sight can be imagined than to see, of a sunny August day, the solans busy at their fishing on the loch. The sun shines on their snowy plumage, throwing them up with great vividness against the dark blue waters. And then their head-long descent, with wings not closed till the moment of entering the water, but pressed tightly back, and the plunge which sends the white spray glistening in the sunlight, are things of great beauty and charm.

On the shores of the Ross there are few days when the sea is not restless. Even into Loch Scridain the Atlantic swell penetrates, and near the head of the loch there stands a rock—Carraigean by name—which acts as a sure index of the state of the ocean beyond. At high water the rock is submerged, but the least swell breaks white here, even when on the shores of the loch no movement is visible. So it is that the landsman crossing, maybe, from Bunessan to the Island of Tiree and passing down the shores of Loch Scridain on his way to the little port, is glad when he sees that all is quiet round Carraigean, or else is filled with anxiety to see the white swell breaking on this lonely rock. And during the winter season with what power does the Atlantic swell beat on these western rocks, even on days when the air is calm and touched with frost. From the high ground of the Ross I have seen the swell dashing in

The Land of the Hills and the Glens

spray on the wild shores of Colonsay—a good twenty miles
from me—so that all the air around the island was rendered
blurred and indistinct by reason of the salt mist that hung
about it. There are days of fierce north-easters, at the
season of spring tides, when the waters are driven westwards
with such force that at low tide great forests of seaweed
stand exposed, and wither in the numbing wind.

In olden days the strip of shore lying between the tide-
marks was often a refuge to the luckless man or woman
who had the ill fortune to have incurred the displeasure
of the fairies and to be pursued by these "silent persons."
For below high-water mark no fairy, nor indeed any evil
spirit, had the power to penetrate, and thus those who fled
before them made their way instinctively to the shore. Of
the fairies many beliefs held good. These little people,
while not actively hostile to man, nevertheless played him
many a sorry trick. Curiously enough, the fairies of the
Island of Mull were said to have only one nostril. Their
dress was usually green, but in Skye they wore clothes
dyed a crotal, or warm brown colour, the dye coming from
the lichen which covers the rocks on the bleak, wind-swept
hillsides. Sometimes they had blue bonnets on their heads.

It is said that on one occasion two men on Iona were
returning of an evening from the fishing, when on their
way they passed the door of a fairy dwelling, or "brugh,"
and saw dancing going on within. One of the men, fas-
cinated by the music which came from the "sithein," joined
the dancers without even waiting to lay down the string
of fish he had in his hand. The other, more cautious, be-
fore he entered stuck a fish-hook in the door—for metal
was a charm against fairy spells—and so was able to leave
when he minded to do so. His unfortunate companion,
however, was forced to remain, and was found twelve
months later—for not until the end of this period was it
possible to release him from the fairy spell—still dancing.
When taken outside by his former companion his fish,

which had till then magically retained their freshness, fell rotten from the string that held them.

This and many other such legends were wont, in the generation that is now rapidly dying out, to be narrated of a winter night around the peat fires of the Ross of Mull while the salt-laden wind howled without, and while within the peat smoke eddied through the room, and the embers glowed in the open fireplace. At such times so worked upon was the imagination of those who listened that they could almost persuade themselves they heard through the storm the wailing of the "ban-sith" or fairy woman, or listened to the thunder of the approach of that other dreaded supernatural being, the "each uisge" or water horse, in his eager search for a victim to ride with to a watery grave.

CHAPTER XXVI

THE HILL BUZZARD

To the eagle, one may say, the buzzard is first cousin. Indeed, from the King of Birds it is not, at first glance, easy to distinguish him, especially at a distance. He has the same flight—though this is not so powerful—as the eagle, and he soars tirelessly, as the latter bird, in the quiet summer air. But against a winter's storm, or in any rough weather, he is unable to rush forward with the strength of the eagle, for he lacks the great power of this bird, and one does not often see him abroad during wild weather.

The distribution of the buzzard is different from that of the eagle. In the central Scottish Highlands, where amongst the highest hills the eagle rears his young, the buzzard is entirely absent. But on the Atlantic seaboard, where the coast is wild and rugged, although the hills are not generally so high as farther inland, the buzzard almost entirely takes the place of the golden eagle now that the erne or sea eagle has been banished from the last of his western strongholds. There is a certain Hebridean island where, along its western seaboard, the buzzard may be seen any day, for here these stately birds are really plentiful, and are but little persecuted, for there is no game-preserving in these wild parts.

It is early in the springtide that the buzzards may be seen at their courtship. One day early in March I passed through a deep glen where several pairs of these birds make their nests. After a night of frost the air was of a wonderful clearness. On the north-lying faces of the lesser hills great icicles showed where the burns had been caught in the grip of the frost. On the higher hills the snow was dazzling

The Hill Buzzard

bright in the sunshine, and to the westward of all lay the Atlantic and her many islands calm and serene. The glen this day re-echoed with the mewing cries of several pairs of buzzards. Sailing through the blue cloud-flecked sky they wheeled and circled, at times swooping earthwards and alighting on some boulder near the swiftly flowing burn, where their tawny plumage could distinctly be seen as the birds stood in the clear sunshine. It was late in April when a pair of these birds chose as their nesting-site a ledge of rock in a narrow ravine. The rocks here were of no great height, and it was possible to walk right into the nest. Here the first week of May I found three speckled eggs, their number and smaller size alone distinguishing them from those of the eagle. The buzzard did not leave her nest until I had almost reached the nesting-ground, when she flapped off, moving her blunt wings vigorously until she had reached an altitude sufficient for her to soar in spirals over the hillside, often uttering her mewing cry, "*pee-u, pee-u,*" the while. Unlike the eagle, she had made little attempt at building a nest, contenting herself with gathering a few twigs of dead heather and tufts of grass. All along the ledge anemones were in blossom, and were actually flowering in the nest itself and close beside where the eggs were lying. I paid several visits to the nest during May and June. The young were hatched out safely and grew apace, though I never found any food at the nest. By the end of June they were well feathered, and took their first flight during the early part of July.

The buzzard is sometimes a late nester, and this points to the fact that, should the first clutch of eggs be destroyed, the birds will lay a second time—a thing which I have never known the eagle do. On one occasion I was shown a buzzard's nest as late as July 3, which contained one solitary chick not more than twelve days old. The nest in this case was situated on a small island where the birds had never before been known to nest, and was built within a few yards

147

The Land of the Hills and the Glens

of the Atlantic on a small cliff. The bell heather was bursting
into bloom as I crossed the moor, and many orchids grew on
the boggy ground. The midsummer sun shone hot and
clear, and the broad Atlantic lay unruffled in the sunlight,
but with a long, oily swell breaking against the rocks.
Twites with their full-grown young rose from the heather,
and wheatears called excitedly from the stony ground, where
their broods had concealed themselves. From the crest of
a small hill sloping down to the sea one could look down
upon the nest and see the buzzard standing on guard over
her young, with the strong sunlight striking upon her. Nor
did she make any attempt to rise until I had approached
nearer, when she flew off mewing and was soon joined
by her mate. And this is a well-marked difference between
the buzzard and the eagle, namely, that the buzzard almost
always cries when she is disturbed from her nest, whereas
the eagle leaves her eyrie in silence. Both birds have the
same heavy, almost clumsy, flight when leaving their nests,
becoming graceful only when they have reached a con-
siderable height, when they can display their fine soaring
powers.

Like those of the eagle, the buzzard's young are, when
first hatched, clad in down of a greyish white. They are
not quite so long in arriving at maturity as the eaglets,
but in all respects closely resemble the latter.

After the nesting season is over and the young are able
to fly, the family of buzzards, accompanied by their parents,
range far over the hills and rough moorland country. Still,
sunny days they love, days when the air is warm and clear,
and when they can soar quietly above the hillsides, all
the time uttering their querulous cry. To the attacks of
other birds they pay no heed, nor do they ever attempt
to escape from their assailants.

NEST OF THE BUZZARD.

Anemones in Flower in the Nest.

YOUNG BUZZARDS,
Nearly Full Grown.

CHAPTER XXVII

THE LOCHAN OF THE WHITE-FRONTED GEESE

IN the wilds of western Ross-shire is a hill lochan where, with the coming of each winter, certain white-fronted geese make their home. The lochan indeed is no more to them than a winter haunt; at the approach of April they become filled with a strange restlessness, and before that month is past they have set out on their powerful wings for their far-off nesting-grounds within the Arctic circle.

This lochan lies on a rough moorland plateau, with deep peat hags to catch the unwary stranger who may attempt a straight course. Across the plateau there stand the relics of ancient forests of Scots fir. Stumps broken off close above the ground and great roots, blackened by the peat, are all that remain of these vast woods, where wolves once had their home and where great stags roamed restlessly in bygone days. But now the climate has changed, and no trees could stand the fierce gales that sweep the plateau in the season of winter.

It was on an afternoon of mid-December that I first saw the Lochan of the White-fronted Geese. In these northern latitudes dusk falls quickly, and the light was already waning as I made my way across the plateau. Beneath me lay the waters of Loch Ewe, ruffled by the breeze, while northward was that part of the ocean known as the Minch, and beyond it again the hills of Harris and the Lewes; their conical summits draped in snow. No sound disturbed the silence of the plateau; no life was visible save where, on the leeward side of a knoll, I disturbed a company of golden plover—or "Feadagan," as they are known in the Gaelic—in their sombre winter dress. As far as the eye

The Land of the Hills and the Glens

could reach no tree nor even bush was to be seen; even the heather was stunted and weather-beaten from many struggles with the forces of the winter gales. But desolate as it was, the scene held that grandeur and beauty which only the country of the hills can give, and so my walk was not a lonely one as I made my way to the lochan.

All wild geese in their habits are most wary of birds, and among their tribe the white-fronted species are no exception to this rule, so that a near view of them is by no means easy. As it happens, however, to this lochan there is one approach, from behind a slight knoll, which, if followed with sufficient care, will lead the naturalist to within a hundred yards of the loch, keeping him all the while entirely hidden from the geese. Having arrived at the top of the knoll, he may, by lying flat on the heather and using the shelter of certain boulders, bring his glass into use and study the birds at leisure, often, though not always, without arousing their suspicions.

On the day of which I write, as I peered cautiously round a large stone, I had the pleasure of seeing a number of the geese standing asleep on a rock which rose from the water near the centre of the lochan. After a time they one by one awakened, dropped into the water, and, having roused themselves from their nap, commenced to feed on some aquatic weed growing in the shallow water. After a while, however, seeming to tire of this, they left the loch, and, walking in single file along the bank, plucked at the brown grasses fringing the shore. All the time one of their number stood motionless on guard, a strikingly alert figure with his white forehead clearly visible against his sombre plumage and the dark background behind him.

At length, as the dusk was deepening, the geese rose in a body from the lochan, and with hoarse cries made their way into the sunset, doubtless setting their course for some other feeding-ground well known to them.

Soon after this day the weather changed, and, with the

The Lochan of the White-fronted Geese

dropping of the wind, the country was quickly in the grip of the frost. But even though no clouds covered the south-eastern sky, it was after nine o'clock this late December morning that the sun rose from behind the snowy top of Ben Airidh Char, and shone clear on the heather of the moorland plateau. Away to the north there lay a mass of billowy clouds, as though heralding squalls of snow from off the cold waters of the Minch. In the sunrise the pale grey of these great clouds became transformed to a faint rosy hue, changing to a deep red colour as the rising sun increased in strength. I have many times, in fine weather, seen this wall of clouds, and they seem to be over Stornoway and the hills behind it—that would be a full forty miles from the "Lochan of the Geese."

No wind disturbed the surface of Loch Ewe this day. On its quiet waters lay a fleet of many herring boats. The previous day at sunset they had set their nets, and were now lifting them, for no herring is foolish enough to be caught in the light of full day. Fishing craft of every description lay there. One saw steam drifters from the East Coast, and with them motor boats, large and sturdy enough, though possessed of little speed. Then there were the small sailing craft belonging to the Highland crofters, and even rowing boats were pressed into the service, for the fishing was good that year, and much money was coming the way of the crofting community through the fishing. Lying at anchor near the pier were the small carrying steamers which were to bear the catches to the port of Lochalsh, a full sixty miles distant, whence they might be sent by rail to the markets of the south. Above the loch the smoke of all these craft lay in a thin blue mist, through which could be seen the long Isle of Ewe, and, away at the entrance to the open sea, where the long swell broke lazily, the dark rocks of Rudha a' Choinn.

The bogs were frozen hard this morning, so that one could set a straight course for the Lochan of the White-fronted Geese, and soon from the shelter of a rock I spied it with the

151

glass. But to-day no geese peopled the lochan; they had been driven forth by the frost which held the waters fast in its grip. Indeed, on the ice one could see their tracks, and they had perhaps kept open a narrow channel as long as possible by continually swimming backwards and forwards.

But with the coming of a south wind a few days later the frost left the plateau, and though on the lochan the ice was by now many inches thick, it was soon melted sufficiently for the geese to return and feed as of old on the succulent weeds.

During the early spring they were still there; but one morning of April, when the breath of spring pervaded the lochan and when the waters of the Minch sparkled blue in the sunlight, the company of white-fronted geese rose with strong cries from the loch, and, rising high into the still air, set their course for the north. Gathering themselves into V-shaped formation, they moved rapidly forward on powerful wings. Past Rudha Stoer, past Cape Wrath, their way led them, and then, crossing far above the Orkneys, they were perhaps over Iceland before the sunset. Here, I think, they halted awhile, for the Arctic was still in the grip of the ice, but immediately their instinct told them that the ice and snow had broken up they pressed forward, for they were making for their nesting-grounds in the high North, where, in Spitzbergen, maybe, or in the Russian tundras, they would rear their young in a land of continual daylight, and would think no more of the Ross-shire lochan till the early storms of autumn warned them that the season of the southward journey was at hand.

CHAPTER XXVIII

THE NESTING OF THE RED-NECKED PHALAROPE

ON certain of the Western Isles the red-necked phalarope has its summer home. It is one of the last of the birds ol passage to make its appearance, and spring has given place to summer ere it arrives. During these days of June, days when the afterglow shows red in the north-east throughout the night—for is not the sun above the horizon till well after ten?—these islands of the western ocean hold much charm. The sea is blue; the hills of the mainland show faintly in the haze, or, maybe, after a day of heat and thunder, when the air is still and clear, they can be seen, sharp and distinct, with black thunder-clouds enveloping their summits, while on the islands the sun still shines, hot and clear. This island of the phalarope, where I first learned to know it, lies well out into the Atlantic.

The island holds in its keeping many lochans. Of these but two are large enough to have the name loch given to them, and it is on the shores of the greater of these two lochs that the phalarope has its home. Westwards the Atlantic is scarcely a thousand yards distant, and when one is near the loch, even in fine steady weather, the swell breaks loud on this shore.

The coming of the phalaropes to their island has never, so far as I know, been marked, but the birds without doubt, make their way northward over the Atlantic, and perhaps halting a while, by the wild sea-girt rocks of Skerryvore and Dubh Hirteach, whence they proceed to their far-distant goal beyond the western horizon.

I shall long remember one cloudless day of June, when I saw for the first time the phalaropes on their native loch. I think the thing which struck me most forcibly at the time was the absence of fear which the birds displayed. As they swam gracefully and easily near the bank, they would allow the human intruder to approach within a very few yards without betraying the least concern, and even then rarely took wing, but swam rather indignantly a little distance away, and then apparently forgot the disturber's presence.

The phalarope is readily identified, even with little experience of its tribe. In size it approaches the dunlin, but is more graceful than the latter bird, and its flight is more wild and swerving. It is, too, distinct from the dunlin, in that it swims habitually, whereas I have never seen a dunlin do so. When on the water the red-necked phalarope rides with extreme buoyancy, and progresses rapidly. Its neck is long and is held erect, and when it approaches the observer the russet-red markings on the cheeks and neck are strikingly handsome. Its call, too, is quite distinctive, a high chirruping cry, resembling no other call that I know of.

Although the phalarope is confiding, the discovery of the nest is by no means easy. I remember how a friend and I spent many weary hours tramping a swamp—with mud reaching to the knee—where we had reason to suppose phalaropes were nesting. But no signs of the birds were forthcoming, and we had almost given up the search when I came upon a pool of water on which a phalarope was swimming buoyantly and gracefully, seemingly without a care in the world. So near an approach did it allow that I managed to get a number of photographs of it at close quarters. It fed almost at my feet, picking off insects with lightning-like rapidity and unerring skill from the leaves of the water vegetation, and occasionally fluttering after a fly or gnat. I certainly did not suspect that it had eggs near, and it was unlooked-for and surprising when it rose quickly and decidedly from the water, winged its way swiftly to a tussock of grass, and, creeping in, settled down on to its nest. Hoping to be able to photograph it while it

The Nesting of the Red-necked Phalarope

brooded, I pressed down some of the grasses, and moved back a few yards. The bird returned to its eggs almost at once, and I could see it endeavouring to conceal itself more effectively, plucking at the grasses with its bill and weaving itself fresh shelter.

Unfortunately for my attempts at photographing it on the nest, I was unable to revisit the spot till the first days of July, and found the young birds hatched, though they were not many hours old. Arriving at the nest, I discovered it to be empty, but the parent birds were moving anxiously around—in marked contrast to their behaviour when they had eggs—and so I waited quietly to see whether the baby family would show themselves. After a while one small downy person emerged from the thick vegetation, shortly afterwards followed by another. Hoping to induce the parent bird to give me a chance of photographing it brooding its young at close quarters, I remained on, and was successful, but in the meanwhile the sun sank, the wind became chill and blew strongly from the west, and I found that one of the small birds was suffering severely from the cold. A crofter's home stood not far distant, so carrying the patient in my pocket, I sought entry there, and held the baby phalarope over the fire. Gradually, from being limp and stiff, life returned to it, and at length I had no small difficulty in holding it, so active were its struggles. At this stage I returned it to its parents, and having done so, moved off from the nesting-site as quickly as possible.

The following year I again visited the phalarope's pool, this time on July 2. The day was fine, clear and sunny. The birds were there as before, one confiding and undisturbed, the other wild and anxious, and flying over the lochan intermittently, uttering excited chirping cries which the mate answered. I gathered that the excited individual was the hen.

After watching what I imagined to be the cock for a while, he disappeared stealthily into a tuft of weeds, and I made certain it was here that the nest was situated, the more so as after the hen, flying over, had called him out, he returned again in a few seconds. However, a most careful search revealed nothing, and a little later on I found what I took to be the nest. The eggs were broken, and must have come to some mischance.

The next day I made my way again to the big loch, and after a long walk came to its shores, and found the charming and varied colony of bird life which it harbours throughout the year. A dunlin still brooded her four eggs, and a colony of terns had each a single egg in their nests; they had probably lost their first and even second clutches, and this was their last effort before the close of the summer. Near the seaward end of the loch I noticed a phalarope betraying great excitement, flying backward and forward in the vicinity of a small pool, and chirruping loudly. I surmised a nest, or perhaps young birds, must be in the neighbourhood, and by good fortune came upon the nest almost at once. It was situated a few inches from the water's edge, and was not concealed so cleverly as the one I had seen the previous year. In it there were four delightful eggs, so characteristic of the phalarope. Very small they were, and compared with those of the snipe, or even dunlin, they were decidedly less pear-shaped, and also, I think, relatively thicker. They were very closely marked with dark brown blotches, which almost hid the ground colour.

Having located the nest I wished to see whether the brooding bird would return to the eggs while I remained in the vicinity, so took up my position not far away, and waited quietly. For some time the phalarope continued its anxious flights, but at length settled on the pool, where it was joined by its mate. Swimming close together and betraying great confidence, they yet lacked the boldness to return to the eggs as long as I remained near them, so I resumed my wanderings, and left them in peace. I was more than sorry, on returning to the loch some weeks later,

The Nesting of the Red-necked Phalarope

to discover that disaster had overtaken the domestic life of the phalaropes. Near the loch the grazing is good, and cattle are constantly feeding there. The beasts usually avoid nests and young birds with noteworthy care, but in this case the eggs had been smashed by a heavy foot, and the parent birds had left the neighbourhood, to return again when the June sun once more shines on their loch.

CHAPTER XXIX

THE LAND OF TIREE

SOME seventy miles north of the Irish coast, and about nine miles to the north-east of Skerryvore, there lies a green and fertile island, Tiree by name.

As to the origin of the island's name much uncertainty exists. The most widely held opinion is that it signifies "Tir-i," or "the Land of Iona," as in olden times the monks were said to get most of their grain from here, and across in the Ross of Mull is a district known as "Pot-i," or "the Larder of Iona," where the monks were wont to obtain their meat.

Another suggested meaning is "Tir-an-eorna," or "the Land of Barley," and a derivation which has of late held favour is "Tir Eadh," or "the Level Land."

Unlike most of the Hebrides, this island is composed mainly of great stretches of level green pasture land lying only a few feet above the height of a spring tide; and, except along its south-west shores, there is none of that characteristic rugged and bleak appearance which is so typical of these western isles.

There is an old saying that "only for paying two rents, Tiree would yield two crops in the season," referring to the extreme rapidity of growth which all cereal crops make on this favoured island, where barley put into the ground in the last days of May is ready for reaping by August, and where the vegetables of the gardens spring up as if by magic. Indeed, so fertile has the island always been, that it bears for its arms a sheaf of corn.

On Tiree the conditions, to my mind, in many ways closely resemble those obtaining on the great plateaux of the Cairngorm Hills. In fine weather these conditions are indeed magnificent, for the sun shines with intense power, and his rays are reflected from the sea with additional brilliance. But of shelter there is none, so that even in midsummer one may vainly seek some protection against the north wind which sweeps down from the Minch, with winter, even at this season, in its breath. And the potato haulms may, even in June, be flattened and rendered black by the gale.

Tiree is famous for its sands. These extend for miles at a stretch, and are of a remarkably white colour, for they are composed entirely of the remnants of shells. When the sun shines on them, their dazzling whiteness is such as to tire the eye, and the dark form of the skua, as he stands in wait for the tern and its catch near the water's edge, seems even darker by contrast. Of all the sands the longest is Traigh Mhor, which extends in a great crescent to a distance of several miles. Here in summer terns glide and wheel, and in winter many shore birds find feeding at the edge of the tide. One sees turnstones, dunlin, sanderling, purple sandpipers, and godwits on this wide shore, while a little way out to sea solans hunt, and long-tailed ducks ride buoyantly. Farther west lies Traigh Bhagh, where terns have their eggs and where the small burn from a chain of lochans enters the sea at its eastern end. Here at times grilse and sea trout attempt to run in from the sea, but there is rarely sufficient water to cover them, so they pass on to the streams of Mull, maybe, or to the far-distant Irish coast. At the south end of the island are the beautiful sands known as "Traigh Bheidhe," from where the dark rock of Skerryvore can be seen, and the tall lighthouse of flashing granite that rises there.

At the extreme south-western end of the island stands the hill known in the Gaelic as "Ceann a' Bharra." Concerning the meaning of this name some uncertainty exists. It may have to do with the fact that from here is a fine view

The Land of the Hills and the Glens

of the distant island of Barra, or perhaps it is a corruption of an earlier Gaelic name given to the hill. But the name, as written at present, is held to be meaningless by a prominent Gaelic scholar. Here the coast is wild and rocky, and the headline precipitous and abounding in caves where rock doves have their nests, and where much driftwood is cast by the tide. After the wind has blown strong from the south-west, the great Atlantic swell thunders on these rocks. Slowly and with a great stateliness the long waves, clear and blue in the sunshine, roll forwards towards the half submerged rocks. They do not break fussily and abruptly as the wavelets of the North Sea or Irish Channel, do these Atlantic giants. Gradually curling over, they crash on the black rocks with tremendous power, throwing the spray high in the air to fall to leeward in a slow cascade of shining whiteness. And when the sun is sinking on the western horizon behind grey storm clouds, and when the ocean wind blows freshly, then it is that on the breeze may be carried the pungent smell of the burning seaweed, coming from Saundaig, maybe, or from Green, and around all the outlying rocks there lies a thin grey mist, arising from the breaking of the great waves, which, despite the wind, seems to hang motionless above the surf.

Many sea birds have their home on Ceann a' Bharra. Here the gentle but somewhat foolish guillemot broods her one egg during the long days of June, choosing as a site for her hostage to fortune a ledge so insecure and slippery that disasters are frequent. Here too the wise razorbill, though in small numbers, finds for her egg a more safe resting-place, usually a cranny hidden away amongst the rocks. Green cormorants are here, too, and from time to time the peregrine and the raven nest in the cliffs, and the grey crow builds her home of the stems of the giant seaweed.

Tradition has it that long ago a party of witches were passing Ceann a' Bharra, on their way to Ireland, sailing, as was their wont, in egg-shells. A native of the island,

A West Highland Crofter's Dwelling

AND

Its Inmates.

A TIREE WOMAN SPINNING.

seeing that his own wife was of the party, and therefore a witch, and knowing that they were in the spell of the evil one, wished them Godspeed on their journey. Instantly the egg-shells were sunk and the man's witch wife drowned.

Fairies were not so long ago held to have their dwellings beneath the grassy slopes of Ceann a' Bharra. These "silent people" were said to come always from the west, for they could pass with equal ease over the ocean as on the land. When travelling they moved in little eddies of wind. When wind and rain came from opposite directions —that is on a sudden change of wind after a shower—it was possible to bring down the fairies in a body by throwing a piece of horse-dung against the breeze.

It is, perhaps, on a clear day of sunshine early in May that Ceann a' Bharra is at its best. By now the grass is springing up fresh and green, and wild hyacinths are tingeing the southern slopes of the hill with blue, while many primroses blossom in the sun-bathed and sheltered crannies, and throw out their scent far across the hill. Away to the east the high corries of Ben More Mull, still deep in snow, throw back the sun's rays, while in the Passage of Tiree trawlers are busy fishing, their mizzens set to steady them in the gentle swell. Far beyond Skerryvore and Dubh Hirteach does the view extend, as far indeed as the track of the big ships, as they make for the Irish coast.

Nestling between Ben Hynish and Ceann a' Bharra is the little crofting township of Ballephuill. Here many of the older generation "have no English," as they quaintly put it, but will greet you in the Gaelic and offer you the hospitality of the Highlander. On the small crofts the land is green and fertile, and then besides the harvest of the land there is the harvest of the sea to keep starvation from the people.

The bracken, or " raineach," as it is known in the Gaelic, is so plentiful and widespread throughout the western coast that it is curious to find it almost entirely absent on Tiree.

The Land of the Hills and the Glens

Only in one spot have I seen it, namely on the slopes of Beinn Hough, a round grassy hill standing on the north-western shores of the island. Still, its absence is no misfortune, for once this quickly spreading fern gains a footing on the land it is extremely difficult to eradicate, and it is not to its credit that it thrives best where the soil is richest.

It is beyond Beinn Hough that there lies the wildest part of Tiree, Craignish Point by name. Here the land runs out, in a narrow peninsula, into the sea, and for miles to the westward there stretches wild broken water, with jagged reefs of rocks where the grey seals rest and round which there swim great copper-coloured lythe of an August evening. A rock-girt coast this, and avoided by mariners except when, in fog or darkness, or helpless in a great storm, their craft approach these great rocks and perhaps meet their end here.

Born and bred by the sea, some of the finest seamen of the west come from Tiree. In their small boats the men put to sea at any time throughout the year when the weather is at all favourable. In summer they are perhaps after saithe, or " piocaich," as they term them in the Gaelic, or they may perhaps be trolling for lythe, for kippering for the winter months. Then there is the lobster fishing, which takes up much of their time from early summer up to December and even to the New Year, should the weather be fair. In winter and early spring there are long lines to be set for cod and ling, and there is also the herring fishing, which of late has brought much money to the island.

Since there is now no peat on Tiree, the natives up to recent years were wont to sail their small skiffs across to the Ross of Mull, over twenty miles to the south-east of the island, where there is an abundance of moss and peat bogs. But more than one accident occurred on the passage across, and more than one boat was lost, so that the custom has been discontinued and coal and drift wood have taken the place of peat.

Lying as it does, well out into the Atlantic, Tiree is visited by many birds during the time of their migration. In the early days of May, whimbrel and white wagtails halt awhile here on their journey north, and many flocks of golden plover, resplendent in their nesting plumage, feed on the grass fields before moving on to the Arctic with swift and powerful flight. Hence the Gaelic proverb, "Cho luath ris na Feadagan," "As swift as the whistling plovers." One season a pair of cuckoos took up their abode on the island for more than a month, so it is probable that the hen bird laid her eggs in some of the many nests of the meadow pipits which breed here. Amongst the children of the island the cuckoos were a source of not a little excitement. The birds were to them quite unknown, and their call was universally a matter for talk.

Amongst the Gaels the cuckoo is spoken of as "Eun sith," or "the fairy bird," and this name has been given to it from the fact that it was said to have its home underground, like the fairies. To this underground retreat it retired on Midsummer's Day—surely rather an early time this for one's winter sleep!—and so was ranked with the wheatear and the stonechat as one of the Seven Sleepers.

In autumn many wild swans visit the island, coming, perhaps, on the arms of a gale from the nor'west, when even the solans have difficulty in facing the squalls, and rise and dip aslant the gale with wings pressed back and stern and grim appearance. The wild swans have great power of flight, and it is a fine sight to see them forging their way, in a line, against the storm, each bird seemingly unaffected by the gale, save that its progress is slower. The first of all the winter migrants to take their departure, the wild swans leave the island during the very earliest days of spring, when, away to the northward, the Coolin Hills of Skye still stand out clothed in a mantle of unrelieved white, and when even the lesser heights of Mull and Ardnamurchan are snowclad.

Later in the season, when full spring is come, the air is at times of a wonderful clearness, and hills at a very great distance are visible. From Tiree to Ben Nevis is a distance of just over sixty miles, yet I have frequently seen this, the highest of Scottish hills, of an early May day, when the mountain was still of an unspotted white and so contrasted vividly with the deep blue of the sky. At such times, through the glass, every rock of the Coolins is distinct, and the hills about Knoydart seem to lose a little of their sternness as the strong sunlight floods them.

I think there can be no island more open to the winds than Tiree. When over in Mull the day has been calm, I have often found a fresh breeze blowing here, and in winter across the island there sweep a succession of gales from the south and south-west, that continue for days without a moment's intermission, so that even the sanderling and dunlin are driven from the sands and the curlew are no longer heard.

Tiree has no safe harbour or anchorage, so that the mail boat is often unable to call, and the island sees its mails and bread being carried off once more to Tobermory or perhaps to Bunessan.

Amongst the older generation of the island it was always held that the wind the old year left behind it would be the prevalent wind for the ensuing year. Thus on Hogmanay, many anxious glances were cast at the sky, and pleasure was expressed if it were seen that the wind was from the south, for the Gaelic saying has it :

" *Gaoth deas, teas is toradh*
Gaoth tuath, fuach is gaillionn
Gaoth 'n iar, iasg is bainne
Gaoth 'n ear, meas air chrannaibh."

The Land of Tiree

Which means:
> " South wind, heat and produce;
> North wind, cold and tempest;
> West wind, fish and milk;
> East wind, fruit on trees."

When on Tiree I have often tested the Gaelic saying that "When the wind is lost, you may look for it again in the south"—"'N uair a bhios a ghaoth air chall iarr a deas i," and have found it almost always correct. Often after a fierce storm from the north the winter's dawn breaks without a breath of wind. The surface of the sea is like glass, yet the sky shows a dull leaden look which portends nothing good in it. Towards midday, or maybe earlier, a puff of air comes away from the south. Within half an hour a fresh breeze is blowing, and before the afternoon is old a whole gale of southerly wind is sweeping up from Islay and the north Irish coast, sending in seas which thunder on the white sands, and causing the herring drifters to seek what shelter they can find. For this reason it is held that the first day of the south wind, and the third day of the north wind, is the best time for crossing the dangerous and tide-swept Sound of Gunna which divides Tiree from the neighbouring island of Coll. But to cross safely one must reach the ferry early even on the first day of the south wind, and I have before now had a wild crossing through arriving at the ferry too late in the day. The tide flows so swiftly here that the wind raises a heavy sea almost at once, and although the ferryman knows every rock and tide rip intimately, it is impossible for a small boat to cross in a storm. But in the summer months the south wind can blow softly and steadily, though at times it may bring with it rains and mist from the sea. Indeed, to the Gael the south wind is sometimes spoken of as "the Gateway of Soft Weather," a poetical expression which has in it a great truth.

No channel that I know of is so frequented by the solan

as the Sound of Gunna. The birds are here throughout the year, with the exception of a short season in the dead of winter, and I suspect that from here they make their way with their catches of herring and mackerel to their great nesting-ground on Borreray, one of the St. Kilda islands, and lying just under one hundred miles to the north-west of Gunna Sound. A long flight this, but nothing exceptional for a bird of so powerful a build as the solan.

In the season of full summer there is little darkness in the Land of Tiree. I have crossed at midnight that great stretch of level land extending across the island from east to west near its centre, and in the dusk have heard the trilling cries of many curlew as they swept in from the sea. From the swampy ground at such times come the curious and pleasant cry of the dunlin and the harsh notes of the corncrake. And before two o'clock (G.M.T.) the song thrushes have been singing their loudest, perched perhaps on the top of some wall, or on some storm-scarred gorse bush, for on Tiree are no trees of any kind. And then the air would be sweet with the music of countless larks, for I think that here, this sweet songster is more plentiful than in any other district that I know, although their numbers are thinned by the fierce peregrine, and their full-grown young have been borne off in my view by herring and black-backed gulls. Then on the "reef" the tribe of the green plover are to be found in their thousands, from early spring to midsummer, and with their peevish cries there mingle the soft melodious notes of the unobtrusive ringed plover, which also have their home here.

And when the strengthening sun has dispelled the early morning mist, how fine a view is to be had away to the east, where the hills of Mull stand in serried ranks! King of them all, Ben More attracts to himself many clouds so that as often as not his summit is invisible even in fine summer weather.

Then, bearing north, Beinn Fada, or the Long Hill,

partly hides the rounded shape of Beinn Talaidh, famous
for the fine grazing on its slopes. Overlooking the Sound
of Mull is Dun da Ghaoithe, only partially seen, and towards
the southern end of Mull, Beinn Buie shows its rock-scarred
summit.

There is the home of the spectre of the Macleans, Eog-
hainn a' chinn bheag, or "Ewen of the Little Head"—a
headless phantom mounted on a black steed, who is heard
riding furiously outside the home of any of the clan before an
approaching death. The ocean is no barrier to this spectre
steed, and the sparks have been seen rising from his feet as
he dashes across the rocky shores of Mull on his way to Tiree.

It is said that during very clear weather the northern
coast of Ireland can be made out from the summit of Ceann
a' Bharra. I have never had the good fortune to see it, but
the distance from this point to Malin Head is not more than
sixty-five miles, so I imagine that the higher hills of that
district should be visible at times.

Since no trees can grow on the wind-swept island of
Tiree, wood is dear and difficult to obtain, so that most of
the crofters' dwellings are constructed of driftwood, carried,
maybe, thousands of miles on the Atlantic tides. To with-
stand the great gales of winter these houses have strong
walls of exceptional thickness, with small windows set in
far back. The old earthen floors have been replaced by
coverings of wood and stone, and one can now very rarely
obtain a " cruisgean " or old-fashioned lamp burning fish oil.

One by one the old beliefs die out—the fairies are now
no more than a name; the water-horse no more inspires a
superstitious dread; the half human, half fairy being known
as the "Glastig" is no more seen abroad of dark and stormy
nights. Yet the natives of this wild island retain all their
charm, and in them the true Highland hospitality and
simplicity is still strong, for their lives are lived close to
the very heart of Nature and they have as their companions
all the four winds and the restful spirit of the everchanging
ocean.   167

CHAPTER XXX

WINTER BIRDS ON THE SHORES OF THE MINCH

WITH the coming of autumn there reach the wild
shores of the Minch many wading birds fresh from their
nesting-homes in the far north. Some of these birds remain
on right through the winter, others again, after a brief
halt, move southward, making perhaps for grassy Islay,
or for the coast of Ireland, where feeding in abundance
awaits them. Many storms sweep the Minch in the season
of winter. From Stornoway across to Loch Ewe is not more
than forty miles, and the islands of the Outer Hebrides shelter
this arm of the Atlantic from the heavy swell from the south-
west. But northward no land lies, and on clear winter
days when the frost holds the land, and when the air
is keen and still, there breaks on the shores a heavy
surf, coming from the north, so that its deep boom may
penetrate far into the country of the wild hills and moor-
lands.

Along the Minch, and alternating with the rocky head-
lands, there lie many beaches of fine yellow sand. Far
different in colour are they from the sands of Tiree, where
shores of whiteness rivalling almost the snow in their purity
throw back the light of the sun so that the eyes are dazzled;
but they possess a charm of their own, and are the haunts
all through the winter months of many birds of the sea
shore.

When the wind is of no great force—a thing rare to
find in this northern land—it is good to lie in the shelter
of the sand dunes and watch the many varieties of birds to
be seen here. None, I think, is more interesting than the
long-tailed duck, or sea pheasant, as it is sometimes

called. These graceful birds do not nest with us—their home is in Iceland and the north of Norway—but any winter's day they may be seen diving energetically for food at a short distance from the shore, and I think they are more assiduous in their diving than even the cormorant. As he submerges the drake throws up the long pheasant-like feathers of his tail so that they are very conspicuous, and, indeed, when flying he always reminds me—the resemblance is more marked in the drake than in the duck—of a pheasant. His flight is none too strong, and his long tail feathers droop behind him as though they were something of a burden.

In their stay under water the long-tailed duck are more or less regular. I have often timed them, and the period of submersion has usually been thirty-five seconds or thereabouts.

I do not know if they are paired throughout the winter: certainly the majority of those I have watched during the days of early January have been mated. Their cry is a low whistling, thought by fishermen to resemble the words "coal an' candle licht," whence it is that in certain parts of the north and eastern coasts the bird goes by this name.

Purple sandpipers frequent the shores of the Minch until, in April and May, they leave for their northern nesting-grounds. No bird is more confiding; indeed, I have often walked up to within a yard or two of them as they were intent on their feeding. Unlike most "waders" they do not keep together in large flocks. A company of a dozen even is a rare thing to see, and usually the birds are met with in twos and threes. Their food seems to consist largely of barnacles, and they are adepts at balancing themselves on wet and sloping rocks, standing in comical attitudes with legs far apart. They rarely swim, but I have once or twice seen one deliberately swim across a narrow channel of deep water. The purple sandpiper is not difficult to identify. Its legs are yellow, of quite a different colour to those of the turnstone, with which it might perhaps be confused, and its reddish bill is black at the tip and light near the base, while spread over its sombre plumage is a slight tinge of purple.

When the wind blows softly so that the swell on the sands is not too heavy, I have watched bar-tailed godwits at their feeding. In appearance they are as miniature curlews, excepting that their plumage is of a lighter colour and the bill, instead of being in a downward curve, has a slight upward tendency. But in their feeding they are far more active than their larger relatives, and constantly probe the soft ooze with their sensitive bills as they walk restlessly about. They seem remarkably resistant to the cold, for I have seen a large flock of them asleep, on a midwinter's day with a cold wind blowing, with the water up to their thighs.

Whereas curlew and godwit frequent the mud flats, sanderling, and to a lesser extent dunlin, keep to the firm sands in their feeding. Of the two latter species the sanderling is the more confiding, specially when he first arrives from his Arctic breeding-ground. In winter plumage he has the breast and underparts of a snow-white colour, so that when the sun shines on the sands a flock of these birds as they stand around resemble, at a distance, miniature sea-gulls. Their great enemies are the black-headed and common gulls, and usually one or two gulls may be seen standing amongst a flock of sanderlings on the feed. Whenever one of the latter birds has secured a morsel and is preparing to eat it, one of the gulls spies him, rushes up, and forcing the small bird to flight, chivvies him here and there in his efforts to make him drop his rightful portion. But the sanderling is an excellent flier, and is much more clever than the dunlin in eluding the tyrant, so that the latter has often to confess himself beaten and retire from the chase.

There is a certain Ross-shire bay where, sheltered from the North Atlantic swell by outlying islands, great northern divers, along with the red-throated divers, are busy at their fishing of a winter's day. No bird, I think, remains under water for so long a period as the true divers. On an average they remain submerged between sixty and seventy seconds, and in that time often progress more than a hundred yards beneath the surface. And with what grace do they dive, making no sound and scarcely a ripple as they go down, nor is it often that they will come to the surface without carrying in their bill some fish or crab—which latter they have at times difficulty in swallowing. Sometimes of a winter's day I have seen the great northern diver, or "loon," as he is sometimes called, flying high and rapidly as he changes his fishing-grounds, and his flight at such times is in marked contrast to his laboured splashings as he attempts, after a heavy meal, to raise himself from the surface of the sea.

There are certain Scottish lochans where the red-throated and even the black-throated divers breed undisturbed, but the great northern diver has never been known to nest in the British Isles, though as late as June 24 I have seen a pair in full breeding plumage in a Hebridean bay.

One of the most interesting birds to watch at its feeding is the turnstone, a wader of about the same size as the red-shank, and with legs fully as red as those of the latter bird. In build, however, the turnstone is more plover-like: its legs are shorter, as is the bill also, and its plumage is more variegated, so that the two birds should never be confused.

Turnstones during the winter are sociable birds, and are generally seen feeding in flocks of considerable numbers. I think I am right in saying that they are almost the only shore bird that feeds independently of the tide. Curlew, godwit, knot, sanderling, dunlin—to name only a few—remain quietly grouped together in some secluded part of the coast-line during the hours of high water, and return to their feeding-grounds only when the mud flats have been left bare by the receding waters. The turnstone, on the other hand, searches actively for food among the seaweed which has been left at high-water mark, so to him the state of the tide is often a matter of supreme indifference. In his feeding the habits of the turnstone are distinctive, and he is well worth watching. The birds generally feed in flocks, hunting with restless activity amongst the "wrack" for the "sand fleas" which lurk therein. They are adepts at turning over the weed, shoving energetically at a heavy mass until they succeed in heaving it over, and then rapidly picking up the prizes that lie exposed. After the passing of the turnstones a line of sea wrack has the appearance of newly-turned hay, for the birds are nothing if not thorough, and search the weed most carefully. Sometimes, though less frequently, they overturn stones; hence, I imagine, their name.

The peregrine at all times haunts the shore lands of the Minch, for his prey is varied here. I remember one winter's day making my way along the rocky coast leading to the remote crofters' settlement of Meal an Udrigil. Mist lay on the hilltops and from time to time grey squalls of driving snow swept across from Ben Airidh Char and the big hills about Loch Maree. Suddenly there passed me, flying at great speed and wildly scattered, a flock of rock pigeons, and after them in hot haste a peregrine, grim of aspect and eager in the chase. The thing that seemed to me most remarkable in this fleeting picture was the fact that a few of the pigeons, lagging somewhat behind the rest, were actually flying at their utmost speed *behind* the peregrine, as though endeavouring to overtake him. Evidently they had completely lost what little sense they ever had, but it looked ridiculous to see them deliberately courting disaster.

From this wild headland it is good at such times to sit in the shelter of some rocky hollow and view the great expanse of ocean and hill country which unfolds itself. Great waves roll in with deep roarings to the high caves, hollow-sounding reports issuing from the caverns as the rush of

Winter Birds on the Shores of the Minch

waters penetrates to their inmost recesses. Long-tailed
duck and scaup ride buoyantly on the rough waters, diving
quickly at times to escape the overfall of an extra huge
wave.

A few miles out to sea lie the Summer Islands, and near
them Eilean a Chleirich, or the Island of the Priest, where
many sea birds have their homes.

Across the waters of the Minch there stand the hills
of Lewis, and there can be seen the entrance to Stornoway
Harbour, a good forty miles distant, with the rounded hills
that guard the port. Away beyond the entrance to the two
lochs—Loch Broom and Little Loch Broom—there stands,
perhaps twenty miles to the northward, the wild headland
of Rudha Stoer, with its lighthouse, built high above the
waters of the Minch. Even at this great distance one can see
through the glass of a clear winter's day the spray rising
high on the rocks as the swell from the north-west breaks,
with the full force of the Atlantic, on this exposed head-
land.

With the coming of spring the winter population of
birds leaves these shores and makes its way northward, but
in its place there come many migrants from the south.
Oyster catchers rear their young on the sandy shores of
the Minch; ringed plovers accompany them, and the sea
swallows make the sands re-echo with their shrill cries.
Then to grassy islands there come the puffins, guillemots
and shearwaters, while in the rocky islets the storm petrel
has its home and the shag and cormorant rear their broods
in the strong summer sunshine, where is wafted the scent
of the sea thrift and of the young fresh grass.

CHAPTER XXXI

THE KELP INDUSTRY IN THE HIGHLANDS

I

DURING the winter months heavy gales, mainly from the west and south-west, force great rollers across the Atlantic, and these, breaking on the outlying reefs and shores of the western islands of Scotland, tear off large quantities of laminarian seaweed. These seaweeds grow mainly just below the limit of an ordinary low tide—though at low spring tides some of their growing fronds are just visible —and fasten themselves to the rocks by means of special root-like attachments known as "haptera " or "holdfasts." The stem of the seaweed varies in thickness, but a good specimen approaches the thickness of a man's wrist, and measures from six to seven feet in length.

This weed, at two distinct seasons of the year, is gathered and burnt, and from the resulting ash, by a chemical process, iodine, potash, soda and other products are extracted.

The history of the kelp industry in the Western Highlands is an interesting one. In many places where to-day it no longer survives great quantities of the ash were formerly produced. For instance, it is said in the statistical account of Argyllshire that on the Island of Ulva, near Oban, one hundred tons of kelp ash were produced annually less than one hundred years ago. To-day not a single ton is made. The Ulva kelp had the reputation of being of excellent quality, and there is an old Gaelic saying to the effect that the Island of Ulva has a harvest of gold about its shores. This saying is now taken as referring to the harvest of kelp which the island formerly provided.

The Kelp Industry in the Highlands

During the Napoleonic wars in the early part of the nineteenth century, the price of kelp, as will be shown later, rose to a very high figure, and at that time quite five hundred tons of the ash were produced on the Island of Mull alone. Gradually the industry declined on the latter island till a few years ago no seaweed at all was burnt there. The work is now being revived to a slight extent, and the tangle is being gathered in a few places in the Ross of Mull, and also on Iona; the western shores of this island retaining large quantities of weed after a storm.

It may be of interest to give an account of the introduction and growth of the kelp industry in these islands.

It appears that as early as 1688 it was realised that the shores of the Orkneys produced "plenty of tangle, of which in other places is made kelp for the making of soap." It was not, however, till 1722 that the first kelp was produced in Scotland, the initial attempt being made in Orkney. At the very first there seems to have been strong opposition on the part of the inhabitants, who considered that the new industry drove off the fish from the coast, and was detrimental to agriculture, in that it deprived the fields of their supply of seaweed manure. The industry was introduced to the Hebrides about 1730, and at first the price obtained for the ash was a very low one—from 18s. to £1 per ton. The value of the product gradually rose, however, reaching the average of over £2 per ton between 1740 and 1760. About this time the industry spread to the Inner Hebrides. It was begun in Tiree in 1745, in the time of the third Duke of Argyll, but the price at first was trifling. It spread to Coll—where, by the way, the industry has entirely died out—in 1754, and was started on Mull in 1768, when the total production of the western coast generally was about five thousand tons. Even at this early period the ash fetched as much as £6 10s. per ton at the glass manufactory of Newcastle. During the remainder of the eighteenth century the price varied considerably, but always with a tendency to rise. The renewal of the war with France had a most far-reaching effect on the kelp market. At this time kelp ash was used in two trades—namely, in the manufacture of soap and glass. The one substance which rivalled kelp was "barilla," the ash of a marine plant called "Salsola soda," and this was imported in great quantities from Spain, since it was of considerably more value than kelp ash. But during the war above referred to the supply was uncertain, and kelp secured the monopoly of the market. The effect of this on the supply of the home product will be realised when it is stated that the price obtained during the three years 1807-9 was four times as great as that realised during the decade 1791—1800.

During the three years above mentioned (1807-9) the great price of £20 per ton was reached, and taking the average of all ash produced in the Highlands a price of £16 per ton was secured. Estimating the total production as 12,500 tons of ash—that is, roughly, no less than 250,000 tons of the wet weed—the sum of £200,000 was realised by the workers during these three years—truly an enormous figure. Largely as a result of this great and profitable industry there ensued a marked increase of population in those districts where kelp making was carried on. For instance, the population of the northern and north-western counties—Shetland, Orkney, Caithness, Sutherland, Ross and Cromarty and Inverness—was 220,411 in 1795. By the year 1831 the figure 287,903 was reached, an increase of 67,492 inhabitants in thirty-six years. The increase was not, it is true, entirely due to the kelp industry, for the expansion in potato cultivation was to a certain extent responsible, but it is noteworthy, nevertheless. In the case of Lewis, Harris and North and South Uist, where much more kelp was burned than in the north and north-western counties, the figures are much more remarkable, for between 1755 and 1831 the increase in the population was no less than 139 per cent., the figure rising from 12,475 in 1755 to 29,934 in 1831.

GUILLEMOTS BROODING THEIR EGGS.

GUILLEMOTS AND YOUNG, IN LATE JULY:
Just Before they Left the Nesting Ledge for the Sea.

The Kelp Industry in the Highlands

Although the three years 1807-9 witnessed the height of the kelp industry, it was not until 1812 that there was any marked decrease in the prices obtained. From 1815 to 1820 the ash still averaged £10 per ton, but after this date the price began to decline rapidly, largely owing to the reduction of the import tax on barilla. This in 1819 was as high as £11 per ton, but by 1823 no more than £5 per ton was levied. The effect of this on the kelp market was very marked, for by 1828 the prices obtained by the home product were less than £5 per ton, and in 1834 as low as £3.

It was not until the middle of the nineteenth century that tangle-ash came to be used for the production of iodine, so it is interesting to realise that during the height of the industry this ingredient, of recent years the most valuable obtained from the ash, was as yet unknown, or at all events, its possibilities were not realised. This new factor steadied the prices somewhat, but so unprofitable had the industry become that by 1875 North Uist had entirely ceased any production, although only some thirty years earlier the neighbouring island of South Uist produced no less than 1,600 tons in a single season. The suspension of so much labour hit the island very hard, and accounted for not a little of the emigration with which the nineteenth century is associated.

In the kelp-making industry as it is now, there are two distinct harvests, the one dealing with the stem, the other with the frond, of the tangle, or laminarian seaweed. That dealing with the stem is the better known and more lucrative of the two. At the approach of winter heavy storms of wind tear from their moorings great numbers of laminarian plants, which are thrown up on the shore. The crofters gather them, and breaking off the fronds, which would merely rot during the long drying process, place the stems in carefully constructed layers on suitable rocks or on stone drying places made for the purpose. These stones should be no more than two feet from the ground, and should support a tangle layer two feet in thickness. Great care must be taken not to allow the tangles to rot during the winter, and for this reason the layers are constructed so that as far as possible the rain water drips off the drooping stems. It is important also that the tangle heaps should be formed out of reach of the spray, and that the stems should be gathered as soon as they appear along the shore. In the choosing of drying places for the tangle stems perhaps the most important thing to be borne in mind is to place them far removed from any stretch of sand.

A well-known chemical company, in more than one of its circulars issued to kelp-makers, prints the sentence, "Avoid sand like poison." It is likewise important that during the burning no sand should become mixed with the ash, for there is nothing that so lowers the price obtained as this impurity. The period of the year during which most tangles are gathered varies considerably, depending as it does entirely on the state of the weather. For instance, during a recent winter there were areas of shore on Tiree where not a single tangle had been gathered even as late as the month of January, owing to the exceptionally quiet conditions which had prevailed during the early winter months. On the other hand the workers on Iona had collected a considerable harvest by the opening days of December. All through the winter and at times even during March and April the tangle stems are gathered. As the power of the sun strengthens the stems gradually lose moisture, until by the end of April or the beginning of May—earlier if the conditions are favourable—they have become hard and shrivelled.

Previous to this time, usually during the early part of March, the stems are removed from the stones where they have lain through the winter and are gathered into heaps in order to protect them from the rain. Here they remain till the first spell of fine weather, when they are burned.

Cattle at times do very considerable damage to the drying

stems. On one occasion on Iona I examined a large pile
of tangles which had been gathered at various times during
the winter, and quite a quarter of the total number had
either been eaten or rendered useless by the trampling of
the animals. At the time I was at the spot some half-dozen
beasts were engaged in chewing the stems, of which they are
extremely fond. It was interesting to note that they did
not confine their attentions to the fresh weed, but consumed
with equal relish stems several months old, which appeared
to the human eye to be far from palatable. It must be dis-
heartening to the workers to see the results of their pains-
taking labours rendered useless in this way.

The fire is set alight with shavings, and perhaps a
sprinkling of paraffin, and once started the withered stems
burn easily, giving off an intense heat. The fire is care-
fully fed every few minutes, as the heap should not be
allowed to burst into flame, and with each armful of fresh
weed a thick, blue smoke with curious pungent smell is
given off. On a fine summer evening these fires dotted
over an island appear singularly picturesque, the blue smoke
curling upwards and being wafted gradually out to sea.
Fine weather is of the utmost importance during the burn-
ing operations, as a fall of rain would seriously impair the
value of the ash.

This retains its heat a good twenty-four hours after
burning, and when thoroughly cool is placed into sacks.
These are collected and placed in a situation where no rain
can reach them, to await the arrival of the steamer which
will carry them to the works of the chemical company,
where the ash will have its more valuable products extracted
from it. About twenty tons of wet tangle stem, or "stamh,"
as it is known in the Gaelic, are needed to produce a ton of
tangle ash.

As regards the dividing of the shore among the popu-
lation for kelp gathering, in Tiree the Duke of Argyll
regulates this by allotting a piece of the shore in each

township to anyone who wishes to make kelp. For this privilege the kelp-maker does not pay anything. The company who purchases the kelp pays a small royalty per ton to the proprietor.

2

THE second part of the kelp industry is the collecting and burning of the fronds of the tangle. Every spring a new frond is produced by the parent tangle plant. It has its growing point at the base of the existing "leaf," and, as it grows, pushes the old frond forward until it separates from the plant. This takes place in April or during the first fortnight in May, and if a period of breezy weather is experienced during this time, great numbers of the fronds are cast up by the tide. The tangle frond is known to the islanders as the "Barr dearg"—the red top—and is gathered as it makes its appearance on the shores. It is carried beyond high-tide mark and is spread over the grass to dry, being "turned" periodically in the same manner as new-mown hay. If the weather remains fine and dry—and this is an all-important factor—the fronds should be sufficiently dry for burning on the third day after gathering. They are then collected in "coles" and burnt on the grass in the same manner as the tangle stems.

Formerly "kilns" sunk in the ground were used for the burning of the "barr dearg," but on Tiree, at all events, these are no longer worked, as it is considered that they produce a temperature so high as to destroy a portion of the iodine. Since iodine is the most valuable product in the ash, it is important that this should be preserved as much as possible. As a result of careful analysis it has been determined that kelp burned in kilns and so formed into a hard slag, gives from ten to fifteen pounds of iodine per ton. Against this the weed burnt in the open fields yields from twenty to twenty-five pounds per ton, and even up to twenty-eight pounds—a striking difference.

The Kelp Industry in the Highlands

On Tiree the fronds are burnt in long strips from twelve to fifteen feet long and two feet wide. The burnt products from the "barr dearg" take at first the form of molten liquid, and care must be used to prevent this liquid from spreading over the surrounding ground. This is effected by burning the fronds in a slight hollow, and along the side of the strip is placed a layer of the wet fronds to keep the liquid within bounds. On cooling, the ash assumes the form of a hard cake, and when broken up reveals many-coloured crystals of great beauty. It is this substance, and not, properly, the ash of the tangle stems, that is known to the workers as kelp.

The ash, then, of both "stamh" and "barr dearg" having been collected and put into sacks, which are provided by the company buying the ash, awaits the coming of the steamer. This vessel is generally a "puffer," which has arrived at the island with a cargo of coal, for "puffers," on account of their construction, are able to put into almost any bay and lie on almost any beach; and such a boat, having discharged its coals, may visit several parts of the island in turn, receiving the cargo of ash from each district.

It is an interesting fact that the industry of kelp-making from the bladder-wrack or "kelp-wrack," as it is sometimes called, has disappeared entirely at the present time in Scotland, though still persisting along the west coast of Ireland. For instance, the hundred tons of kelp which were at one time produced on Ulva were extracted almost entirely from the bladder-wrack; now the industry is a memory only. The same thing applies to many of the sea lochs and sheltered sounds of Argyll. Here the laminarian weed grows sparingly, and the swell is never sufficiently heavy to cast it up on the shore, so that the kelp ash formerly made was produced entirely from the bladder-wrack. In the Craignish district, for example, a considerable amount of the kelp-wrack ash was formerly produced, and also on some of the more land-locked lochs of Mull, as, for instance,

The Land of the Hills and the Glens

Loch Spelve. The labour entailed in gathering the bladder-wrack, or *Fucus,* was greater than that necessary for the collecting of the tangle. The wrack was not cast up by the sea in sufficient quantities for the requirements of the industry, and had to be cut as it floated in the water, the workers using boats for the purpose. It is, therefore, a fact of no little interest, and one which must be borne in mind when the revival of the kelp trade is under discussion, that the weed which was almost entirely used when the industry was at its prime, one hundred years ago—the *Fucus* or bladder-wrack—is now held to be of so little value that it is no longer worth exploitation. It will readily be seen that this affects the revival of the industry along the more sheltered parts of the coastline, where the tangle is uncommon as compared with the kelp-wrack of earlier days. The reason for this change in the material used is the fact that the products extracted from the kelp ash a hundred years ago have now been superseded in the manufactures in which they were formerly used. During the height of the kelp boom, as was pointed out above, the ash was mainly employed in the making of glass and soap, seaweed being then practically the only source of soda, which is necessary in the manufacture of soap. But the discovery of the Leblanc process of making soda and the repeal of the salt tax with the lowering of the import duty on barilla, caused the disastrous fall in the prices which, it was thought, would at one time cause the industry completely to die out.

The prices obtained, even over a small area, vary considerably, so much so that the natives sometimes draw lots for the best "beat." Thus the tangles washed up on sandy beaches fetch, may be, no more than one-third of the price obtained from the weed gathered from rocky or shingly shores not more than a hundred yards away, on account of the grit which attaches itself to them and which later on contaminates the ash.

A point to be remembered is that the industry is one

The Kelp Industry in the Highlands

which can be profitably combined with small holdings, of which many have been established of late on the islands. The season of the tangle gathering is when work on the croft is light, and the burning of the weed can be held over until after the spring crops have been put in. With regard to the collecting of the fronds, these, perhaps unfortunately, are washed ashore usually at the season when the small-holder is busy with the land, but at that time of the year the days are long, and there should be little difficulty in gathering a considerable quantity of this part of the weed also. The price obtained from the ash of the "barr dearg" has not risen proportionately to that of the tangle stems during the last few years, so that the latter form the main industry.

Although it is to be feared that the islands will never again see the record prices of a century ago, the present time is undoubtedly one during which the resources and capabilities of the industry should be strengthened in every possible way, so that kelp making in the Highlands and Islands may be put on a prosperous footing, and the supply be so good that it may be able to hold its own against foreign competition.

CHAPTER XXXII

SPRING IN·THE WESTERN HIGHLANDS

I.—MARCH

MARCH came in this year with bitter cold, carried down by a strong north-easter. Even on the sea-girt islands the ground was frost-bound, and the lochans, even where full open to the wind, were frozen across. Below the snow-line the heather and hill grasses were remarkably dry, and heather fires, some of great extent, were everywhere to be seen.

On March 9 a raven's nest in a small east-facing rock was visited. The birds were in possession, but I do not think any eggs had been laid. The ravens sailed round, flying so close as almost to touch one another. One of them called frequently in a high note, resembling more the call of a full-grown young raven than the usual deep croak of the adult bird. On March 18 a raven's nest, built in a cliff only a few yards from high-water mark, contained no fewer than seven eggs, and the nest referred to in the first instance also contained eggs at this time.

The common gull, though found along the western sea-board through the winter, is largely a summer visitor, in that those birds breeding along the West of Scotland spend the winter in more southern latitudes. These birds arrive in large companies, and for some weeks keep together, haunting the ploughed fields in the vicinity of the sea lochs and following the plough, before withdrawing to the isolated islets where they nest. On March 17 I saw the gulls for the first time, and their loud cries as they wheeled together over the land like a shower of driven snow, were good to hear after the winter's quiet. It is not until the early days of May that the common gulls commence their nesting, or even later should wintry weather continue.

Lapwing are for the most part still going in flocks as I write (April 1), and the dunlin have not yet paired, nor have they left the sands for their inland nesting haunts. A small company of about a dozen purple sandpipers which have frequented the rocks throughout the winter and which seemed to have disappeared towards the end of February have again been seen throughout March, the last occasion I noted them being on the 27th. On the 12th I saw one deliberately walk into deep water and swim from one rock to another a distance of at least fifteen feet. About the same time I saw a turnstone do the same thing, but as far as my experience goes it is very rarely that either of these birds deliberately goes out of its depth. Mergansers have increased during the month and are now common. On March 19th I saw three greenshank feeding on some soft ooze, and in the mud their movements seemed strangely laboured. On the 23rd I visited a favourite shore resort of curlew, and although the weather was summer-like, the birds were not uttering their spring call. This, I think, seems to show that they must be birds which nest much farther north than Britain, for the local birds were already on the moorlands and using their full spring notes. Large flocks of knot still frequented the mud flats, the sunlight glinting on their plumage as they swerved and wheeled in restless but well ordered flight. Near them were more than fifty shelduck, perhaps resting on their northward migration. In flight they are heavy and resemble geese rather than ducks. During most of the time I had them under observation they dozed in the warm sun, but occasionally took short flights as they changed their feeding grounds. The ringed plover were all pairing.

By the end of the month gannets were numerous in the waters surrounding their nesting rocks and guillemots were moving in from the deep waters.

March 26 was the most wintry day of the whole season.

The Land of the Hills and the Glens

Snow fell in dry powdery flakes, accompanied by a gale from the west, and much drifting took place on the hills, so that the road at the head of the glen was blocked for some days. The next day was clear and sunny, and I saw the first wheatear, looking cold and uncomfortable.

2.—APRIL

By the first of the month quite a number of wheatears had arrived at their nesting-grounds. The weather was now mild and sunny, and indeed throughout the month there were few wintry spells, although a good deal of rain fell and there were strong winds from a westerly quarter.

On the first of April I visited a raven's nest built on a ledge of rock not more than fifteen feet from the ground on a heather-clad hillside sloping away from a sea loch. The nest was facing north-east and was in an exposed position, but this notwithstanding, the young were just hatching out. I was unable to look right into the nest, but with a stick could feel the soft bodies of the chicks and the remaining eggs. One would have imagined that the parent birds would have displayed great anxiety at such a time, but they appeared singularly indifferent, and did not approach anywhere near when I was at the nest. I noticed one bird apparently feeding the other on a knoll a few hundred yards away.

That evening I visited a dipper's nest built in a niche of rock above a waterfall. The nest was fully built, but I could not tell whether the bird was sitting, as it was impossible to approach the nest itself.

On the third, the fine weather continuing, I crossed to one of the islands, and for the first time this year saw numbers of Manx shearwaters gliding with picturesque flight above the surface of the sea. No puffins, apparently, had arrived as yet, but the common gulls were everywhere, and the green plover were commencing to nest.

YOUNG GOLDEN EAGLE IN THE EYRIE.

The Hindquarters of a Hare lie in the Foreground.

YOUNG FULLY-FLEDGED GOLDEN EAGLE,

Showing the conspicuous White Markings on the Wings.

Spring in the Western Highlands

On the fifth the curlews in the big glen were uttering their spring call, and by this time, too, stags—the more forward of them—were commencing to shed their horns. Thrushes and blackbirds are late in commencing to sing along the western seaboard, and it was not until April 8 that they were in really full song.

Much burning of tangles for kelp was done during the fine spell, the pungent odour of the smoking weed travelling far across the islands.

In the early mornings the blackcock were fighting regularly and industriously, and also to a lesser extent after sunset. Over the birch woods many woodcock flew of an evening with curious bat-like flight, uttering from time to time their grunting cry and their sharp hissing note, "*chissick, chissick*." The hen birds are at this time brooding their four speckled eggs—for the woodcock is one of the earliest of nesters—and this evening flight seems to be undertaken by the cock birds only and may be a kind of display.

Much heather was burnt during the first week of April; and, taken all through, this spring has been an exceptionally favourable one along the western coast for this purpose.

A pair of redshank nesting amongst some tussocky grass near the sea were much in evidence about the tenth of the month. The eggs had not yet been laid, and the birds were courting, the male flying up into the air and sailing earthwards, continuously uttering his flute-like whistle. Curlews about this time were everywhere on the hillsides uttering their trilling cry, especially before rain.

By the thirteenth of the month the larch woods in the more sheltered situations were budding, the rich red flowers showing in profusion. Missel thrushes were sitting, and stonechats also had eggs by this time.

On several occasions I noticed about this time a barn owl abroad and hunting in full daylight. I believe he had his nest in a neighbouring wood, but I did not succeed in discovering it.

On April 21 I visited a small island on which a large colony of common gulls nest. A few nests appeared to be completed, but I did not see any eggs, for it was somewhat early for these. The solitary eider duck, which usually nests on the island, had not as yet arrived, nor had any of the red-breasted mergansers.

On April 22 I visited a heronry and found young birds in one or two of the nests—one brood being at least ten days old. The weather this day suddenly changed from very clear and sunny conditions to heavy squalls of rain and sleet, which fell as snow on the high grounds. On the 27th, with little warning, the weather turned quite summer-like. On this day I saw the first sandpiper, common tern, swallow and sand martin, and heard a willow warbler in song. On the 29th whimbrel were passing over, and on the 30th I heard a whinchat in song. The temperature on the last two days of the month exceeded 65 degrees, and the snow-fields rapidly dwindled even on the higher hills. Everywhere the birches were budding and the air was filled with the sweet aroma from their young leaves.

3.—MAY

THE cold and unsettled conditions prevailing during the earlier part of the spring having come to a close with almost bewildering suddenness during the last days of April, summerlike weather prevailed at the opening of May.

Blackcock still fought regularly at their chosen grounds at the beginning of the month, and on the morning of May 2, between four and five o'clock, I watched for some time a number of these birds.

I saw the first puffins on the morning of May 2. These birds seem to be already paired when they arrive at their summer quarters, and it is a curious fact that, although numbers of them are thrown up dead on the beach after a winter storm, I never once saw a specimen at sea from September till the opening days of May. On May 2, also, numbers of white wagtails were feeding on the short grass above the high-tide mark, and for the next week were present, though it is possible that the earlier arrivals were succeeded by later migrants during this period. The white wagtail does not nest in this country except in one or two isolated localities, and the migrants which are seen along the western coast line during the early days of May are probably on their way to Iceland.

On May 3 I saw the first whimbrel, and in the afternoon of the same day watched a flock of these charming birds coming in from the sea. Their course was from the south-east, and I think there is little doubt they were on migration. For the first part of the month they remained on the island, and as late as May 20 stragglers were still with us. When first they arrived they permitted a near approach, and were reluctant to take wing unless obliged to do so. Their behaviour thus contrasted strongly with that of their wary relatives, the curlew. Apart from their smaller size, there is little to distinguish the whimbrel from the common curlew, but the call note at once determines the species. The usual call note of the whimbrel is a couple of short, sharp whistles, quickly repeated and sounding something like " *tety, tety, tety,*" the notes being more abrupt and jerky than those of the curlew. Besides their common call whimbrel utter a long-drawn, plaintive whistle like a curlew's, and also a vibrating call resembling that of the curlew, only more subdued, and, I think, more liquid. It does not nest with us except as a straggler, but farther north it largely replaces the curlew, being common in the Faroes and Iceland.

Up to the middle of May dunlin and sanderling still frequented the coastline, the dunlin in some cases having assumed the full breeding plumage. The dunlin nests on the island of which I write, but those seen along its coast in May are making their way to northern nesting-grounds, perhaps within the Arctic Circle. Though a bird, during the nesting season at all events, of similar habits to the common snipe, the dunlin does not lay her eggs till the snipe's young are active birds. Indeed, on May 4, when I visited some boggy ground where quite one hundred pairs of dunlin nest every season, the birds, except for one or two individuals, had not even arrived, much less commenced the duties of rearing their offspring.

Golden plover were still here in flocks during the early part of May, on their way to their northern breeding-grounds, the birds strikingly handsome in their full nesting plumage.

The peregrine falcon is a bird which suffers such persecution at the hands of keepers that I was glad to discover on May 8 a nest of this handsome hawk containing three eggs. The nesting site was the summit of a high sea cliff, and the male peregrine, at my approach, betrayed the fact that he had a mate near by flying off his perch on the rock and uttering his harsh note of alarm repeatedly. The hen bird then emerged, mingling her cries with those of her mate, and I was able to reach the nest, somewhat unexpectedly, with little or no climbing. The eggs were laid under a stone just on the top of a sheer cliff, and at my visit the young birds were chipping the shells.

It was on May 3 that I saw and heard the first corncrake, an early date for this migrant. There was as yet little or no grass, so the bird had perforce to hide itself in a clump of gorse bushes. By the end of the month the fields of growing grass resounded throughout the night with the grating notes of many corncrakes.

Curlew and redshank commenced to brood during the first week of May, and one nestful of curlews hatched out on May 29. Though the eggs were chipped as early as the

26th, the young birds did not fully emerge till three days later. In a country where grey crows and gulls abound every bird has to keep a watchful eye on her eggs, and the parent curlews in this case attacked with ferocity any winged marauder venturing in the neighbourhood of their nest.

Oyster catchers, most regular birds in their nesting, had eggs about May 10, which was, I should say, from two to three days later than the previous year. One nest I found contained two eggs which were quite remarkable. They were not more than one-half the usual size, and indeed closely resembled the eggs of the common tern, except that the shells were rougher and thicker. Unfortunately the eggs disappeared—they were, I think, eaten by gulls—so it was not possible to observe what manner of chick emerged from such abnormal eggs. Another oyster catcher had an unpleasant experience. Last season she laid her eggs and hatched her young in a field of young oats fringing a sea loch. This year the field was under potatoes, so I was surprised to see that she had again chosen it as a nesting-site and had laid her eggs on the crown of a furrow. The field shortly afterwards was harrowed, and in the process one of the eggs was broken and the other two thrown to the bottom of the furrow. It says much for the devotion of the parent bird that she continued to brood on the couple of mud-encrusted eggs in their new situation, though she made no effort to make a nest around them.

Terns were, I think, rather later than usual in arriving. As late as May 15 I passed an island which is a specially favoured nesting-site, and not a single tern had arrived. It was not until May 19 that I saw the first birds. The nightjar, perhaps the last of our summer migrants to arrive, was heard for the first time on the evening of May 24, and the following evening I had an excellent view of the bird as he sat on one of the fence posts just outside the window, uttering his low and curious call note. This may be likened to a loud, low-pitched purring of a cat, only on two notes.

On May 31 a severe storm of wind and rain visited the Western Highlands and brought the rivers down in great flood. Young grouse were hatching about this time, and in all probability numbers succumbed.

RAZORBILL APPROACHING **HER** EGG.

RAZORBILL BROODING.

Her Egg is on an Exposed and Narrow Ledge—an Unusual Situation.

CHAPTER XXXIII

SUMMER IN THE WESTERN ISLANDS

I.—JUNE

DURING the month of June the weather was almost uniformly cold, and from midday on the 1st till the 21st of the month the wind blew steadily from the north. For the first thirteen days the shade temperature did not once reach 60 degrees, and on the 12th the northerly wind reached gale force. For fully ten days Ben Nevis was covered with an unbroken coating of fresh snow, an unusual event so late in the season.

On June 1 the majority of the curlew had hatched out their young and the oyster catchers were sitting hard. It is interesting to notice how conservative this latter bird is in the choice of a nesting-site, returning each season to the same stretch of shingle and laying her eggs within a few feet of the site occupied by her the previous year. On June 2 I saw what seemed to be a pure white oyster catcher fly past, accompanied by its mate. On that day I watched for some time a starling energetically searching for food amongst the seaweed. Her nest of youngsters was among some "scree" up a very steep hill face, and I noticed that the bird on her journeys back to the nest with food did not fly straight up the hillside, but followed a zigzag course.

On June 6 I again visited the peregrine's eyrie. The young falcons were now about twenty-seven days old. Originally there were three eggs, but only two young were reared. These, at the age of a month, were fine heavy birds, with some of the white down still adhering to them. During the time I was at the vicinity of the nest both parent birds kept up a continuous screeching. Although there was no fresh prey in the eyrie, the bones and mummified remains of many

193

birds were lying around, yet kittiwakes and cormorants brooded on their nests on the rocks, paying no heed to the agitated peregrines soaring overhead.

During the first week of June Arctic skuas still frequented a stretch of shore some distance from their breeding-ground, the continuous north wind probably retarding their northward migration. On one occasion I saw a tern being hotly pursued by a skua, while the tern's mate was in its turn attacking the aggressor. As late as June 8 I saw a flock of dunlin in full breeding plumage frequenting the shore, and about this time noticed a small island crowded with eider drakes. These birds are not by any means model husbands, for they leave their wives when the latter begin to sit, and take no further interest in their families.

At the beginning of the second week in June the young of numerous tree pipits and whinchats were hatched out, and at this time most of the oyster catchers had chicks, betraying great anxiety when their nesting-haunts were approached. Ptarmigan are few and far between in the Western Highlands, and it is not by any means easy to locate one of their nests. On June 14, the first warm day of the month, I was on the high ground, and at a height of a little over two thousand feet a cock ptarmigan rose. A few yards from where he had been sitting the hen bird rose from her nest, containing four strikingly beautiful eggs of a rich red colour. The eggs were freshly laid, and judging from the smallness of their number and the late date—ptarmigan usually begin to brood during the third week in May—I think this was a second laying. Rather later in the day, just over the hill-top and sheltered from the wind, I watched a ptarmigan with a fine brood of eight chicks only a few days old. On becoming suspicious the old bird called to her family with a strong, high-pitched cry, when they immediately ran to her, scrambling ludicrously over the stones and following her at top speed over the brow of the hill.

A surprisingly large number of gulls were to be seen

on the high grounds on this day. Common gulls, herring gulls, black-backed gulls—all passed overhead, and it seems noteworthy that any ptarmigan is able to preserve her eggs or young intact when so many enemies are abroad. Once a golden eagle soared past me not many yards away, seeming incongruous among the company of sea-birds, and later I saw it mobbed by a gull and some species of hawk.

Plant life of the hills suffered from the continuance of the high and cold wind. The cushion pink (*Silene acaulis*) did not bloom before mid-June, and at that time even the violets were still in flower on the higher ground.

On June 15 a pair of wood warblers had baby young in an oak wood by a burn-side, and about this time a family of dippers left their nest in the cleft of a rock overhanging a waterfall. Red-breasted mergansers—the latest of the duck tribe to nest—commenced to brood about the 15th, and on one small island I counted three nests.

Right up to the end of June curlew continued to make use of their musical vibrating cry, and on June 20, a day of mist and gloom, I heard them calling more strongly and wildly than I ever remember. And there are few cries so full of pathos and feeling, and the spirit of the wild places, as the call of the curlew.

2.—JULY

THE cold northerly type of weather experienced almost continuously throughout June was again prevalent during the first fortnight of July, but after the 17th of the month winds from a southerly quarter prevailed, with some very warm weather from the 21st to the 28th.

Perhaps the most noticeable feature of bird life during the month was the complete disappearance of the terns from islands where last season they nested in their hundreds. Their absence is to be regretted, for of an evening com-panics of terns fishing round the shore line are always of considerable interest to the bird lover.

During the early days of July a colony of Arctic terns had laid their eggs along a stretch of shingle, yet at the close of the month, when I repassed the locality, not a single bird appeared to have young. The majority of dunlin had hatched off their young by the first week of July, and displayed their usual anxiety for their progeny, uttering their rasping cries, and at times feigning injury in their efforts to draw off the intruder from the vicinity.

Red-necked phalaropes were still brooding their eggs during the first days of the month.

After a succession of dull, misty days during the middle of July, the morning of the 21st broke with a dense white fog lying thickly over the water and the lower grounds. Above this blanket the hills rose with fine effect, appearing as islands rising from the mist-sea, and, topping them all, Ben Nevis showed more clearly than I ever remember. As the sun increased in strength the vapour was dispelled, and the day was the warmest experienced up to this time during the summer. For a week the weather continued intensely warm, with a shade temperature verging on 80°, and the sun shining with great power.

On July 25 I crossed a favourite nesting-ground of the lapwing, and although the great majority of the young birds were strong on the wing, certain nestlings were still being tended by their parents, who showed considerable alarm when their nesting-ground was invaded. Although dunlins had eggs as late as the commencement of July, a search through two breeding-places on the 25th and 26th revealed the presence of only one dunlin which showed any anxiety when approached, and not a few of the birds were already frequenting the coast-line in flocks. At the end of the month I saw what I took to be a full-fledged young phalarope, able to fly without much difficulty.

I have always felt that in their nesting the common and

Summer in the Western Highlands

Arctic terns are the most unfortunate of birds; many of their first clutches of eggs are stolen from them, either by gulls or hooded crows, or else by the hand of some small boy. As late as July 25, on visiting a small colony of Arctic terns on the shore of an inland loch, I saw four nests, each containing a single egg, and I doubt much whether the colony had, up to that time, succeeded in hatching off a single young bird. On the same day I somewhat unexpectedly came across a colony of perhaps twenty pairs of lesser terns, on a stretch of shingle running down to the open Atlantic. As I neared the colony a company of grey crows, feeding on a carcase thrown up by the tide, passed close to the terns in their flight from me, and instantaneously the small terns gathered in a body round their deadly enemies, swooping furiously at them until the crows were away from their neighbourhood. Some of the lesser terns still had eggs, others newly hatched young, and the parents of these latter stooped angrily at me, uttering chattering cries.

During the last week of July very few meadow pipits still tended their young, but oyster catchers and sandpipers showed great anxiety over their broods, and the young of the merganser were even then in the downy stage. Isolated corncrakes still called from the now luxuriant fields of hay, and at least one pair of curlew had young small enough to cause them acute anxiety when I strayed on to their nesting-ground. On July 27 I crossed a stretch of boggy moorland where numbers of Arctic skuas nest every year. Some of the birds must still have had young but they were noticeably silent. Indeed, only twice did I hear an individual call.

The gannet, or solan goose, was late this season in making its appearance on this part of the western seaboard, on account, I think, of the cold weather and consequent tardy appearance of the mackerel and other fish, but is now plentiful. While at sea I passed a solan sound asleep, and so gorged that it quite failed in its efforts to rise from the water, calling angrily at us in its helplessness as we passed. One rarely sees a solan mobbed by other birds, but recently I noticed one whose flight took it past a stretch of coast marked out by a greater black-backed gull as its own domain. The gull pursued the solan a considerable distance out to sea, and when it gave up the chase the solan alighted on the water as though exhausted.

Towards the end of the month large flocks of curlew had arrived from the north, and while at sea on the 25th a swift passed us going south, but not till next month does the full tide of bird migration set in southwards.

3.—AUGUST

DURING August, wild life is not so evident as in the preceding months. Most of the birds have reared their broods ere now, and are in process of moulting, so that they avoid human observation as much as possible.

One of the earliest birds to reach us from the far north is the purple sandpiper. Unlike most of the waders which appear in flocks, this sandpiper is usually seen singly or in pairs, and is usually a bird of silence, uttering no alarm note as it flies stealthily away. Dunlin and golden plover arrive in their hundreds along the mud flats, and curlew from the north now take the place of the home nesting birds, which in their turn move on southwards. The common gulls, which nest so plentifully on the grassy islands of the West Coast, disperse from their nesting sites, and they, too, pass south. The common sandpiper is one of the first of the summer migrants to depart, for it remains on only till its young are strong on the wing. During the first week in August these birds leave quietly and unobtrusively—one does not see their going, but one day their graceful forms are no longer to be seen flitting across the water, and it is realised that they have started off on their long journey.

In the opening week of the month oyster catchers in some

Summer in the Western Highlands

instances had comparatively small young, though these must have been the result of a second brood, and eider duck still had young in the downy state.

Most variable weather conditions were experienced during the first ten days of August. On the 1st there was a heavy rainstorm and wind from the south-west, and from the 4th to the 11th there was thick fog almost daily. On land the mist usually disappeared about midday, but over the sea it remained in the form of a dense white cloud, on which the sun shone brightly. Shipping was much interfered with during this period, and on the western coast this fog was held to be the most dense and persistent experienced for many years.

Stonechats were tending their second broods through August, showing the usual symptoms of alarm when their "beat" was approached. A certain pair of buzzards were still feeding their young in the early days of the month, in the face of a rock on a wild plateau over one thousand feet above sea level and overlooking the Atlantic. On the 10th I put up a snipe with a young bird beside her, scarcely able to fly. These very late broods of the snipe are not unusual, for they seem, like the woodcock, to rear a second brood when the summer is well on.

Willow warblers, after their silence in July during their autumn moult, were in song again in early August, though as a rule their vocal efforts were feebler than earlier in the season. The last I heard was on August 19, and his song was strong out of the ordinary for so late in the summer. On that date, too, I saw a migration of missel thrushes and ring ouzels, the birds resting on the banks of a hill burn on their journey south. Even as late as the last week of the month some of the merganser broods still consisted of quite small birds.

The last days of August were remarkable for their wonderful clearness and for the contrasts in light and shade which they produced. In some districts tropical showers fell, but cleared away soon, and never do I remember seeing the hills so strikingly beautiful, with their slopes bathed in sunlight, while on their summits great black clouds hung. Bird life revelled in the clear fresh air, and at one time I saw a family of three buzzards and four or five kestrels wheeling and dashing madly through the air above a giant cliff overlooking the broad Atlantic.

Such days as these are rarely experienced and live long in the memory.

CURLEW BROODING.

Beside the Bird can be seen the Head of one of her Chicks.

CURLEW APPROACHING HER NEST.

CHAPTER XXXIV

AUTUMN IN THE WESTERN HIGHLANDS

I.—SEPTEMBER

THROUGHOUT the whole of September an unsettled type of weather conditions prevailed. The month was ushered in with a gale from the west and a heavy sea, and strong winds from every quarter continued almost uninterruptedly till the closing days of the month. The harvest was late on the West Coast, though the crop as a rule was excellent, and it was not until the end of the month that the bulk of it was secured.

During September solan geese were more plentiful around the sea lochs than at any time during the summer, and on the 18th, during an exceptionally heavy gale from the north-west, I noticed them fishing in a little land-locked bay, into which they do not venture under ordinary conditions.

In the first fortnight of the month many sea birds were migrating. I saw flocks of kittiwakes far out to sea, wheeling and fluttering above the waves, and strikingly white did they look as the sunlight glanced on their plumage, contrasting strongly with the dark blue of the waters beneath them. Great shearwaters, with their lesser brethren the Manx shearwaters, were going south about this time, and a few fulmar petrels were to be seen. Flocks of phalaropes, with swift, swallow-like flight and twittering cries, were also on migration. A certain number of grey crows visited us at this time, though the flood of their migration strikes rather the East Coast than the West. But then on the West Coast there is always a large resident population of these birds, so that it is not easy to mark an additional influx of migrants.

Ravens are always present along the high cliffs which border the Atlantic, and even during September one saw them turning over on their backs in mid-air—a performance which is associated with the first months of the spring rather than the early autumn. There is nothing, I think, that birds of powerful flight—raven, peregrine, buzzard—like so much as to soar against a breeze, moving just above the top of a high cliff, and using the uprushing current of air to their own advantage. The same pair of birds may time and again make their way along the same route, wheeling off when they have reached a point where the wind no longer assists them, and returning on a different line.

Towards the end of the month the lapwings of a Hebridean island where thousands breed had to a certain extent collected into flocks, but many were to be seen in pairs, and I frequently observed such birds wheeling and dashing across the fields in that wild, buoyant flight which is characteristic of their mating season. They also practised their spring notes, and somersaulted in the usual mating fashion. I have not known them to do this before at the autumn season of the year.

This island is the home of many birds. It is never quiet, for at all times of the year the birds rest on its shores, and fill the air with their cries. During the last days of the month the wind blew from the east—not a favourable wind for migration—yet the shores of the island were already thronged with waders from the far north. There were bartailed godwits—birds of slender build and reminding one of a whimbrel—which were more confiding than the curlew, and searched for food among the sea wrack, flying off when approached too closely, with shrill, piping cry. One saw flocks of ringed plover with a few dunlin among them; but, curiously enough, not a single *flock* of dunlin was observed. Sanderlings there were in plenty; they had kept together in large flocks, usually haunting the water-line, but at times feeding on the grass above high tide. Knot were scarce, and I saw these birds on two occasions only. They were with dunlin and ringed plover, and their larger size and flight, somewhat like that of a golden plover, made them easily recognisable.

Where seaweed-covered rocks broke the continuity of the sand turnstones were to be seen, and on the fields fringing the shore the plaintive whistle of the golden plover was usually to be heard. Once I disturbed a greenshank from a boggy creek, and he flew off, uttering that wild note of his which cannot be mistaken for that of any other bird, and which always recalls to the mind wide moorlands and pine woods, where the bird makes his home in the season of nesting.

A few wheatears remained at the close of the month, but the majority had gone south. Twites were in flocks, and the forerunners of the hosts of widgeon had already arrived on the lochs. The last days of the month were beautifully fine and calm, and one afternoon I watched starlings in their hundreds acting as flycatchers, and soaring into the air after the many insects that were disporting themselves in the sunlight. On the 28th I was surprised to see a turtle dove feeding on a stubble field—surely this bird must be an uncommon visitor to the Hebrides—and that same day I saw a peregrine swooping down on some lapwings which were migrating.

The last evening of the month brought a sunset of wonderful beauty, the sun sinking behind an unrippled sea, and even the distant islands appearing close at hand. One felt the touch of autumn clearly on this day, but summer lingers long beside these islands of the Atlantic, and will not finally leave them for some weeks to come.

The Land of the Hills and the Glens

OCTOBER has been a month with an unenviable record, for it brought with it weather which, for its wildness, has not been equalled during living memory. And yet its opening day was of midsummer warmth, with a sky of deep blue and flecked with white fleecy clouds, and not the veriest trace of a swell on the surface of the Atlantic. I remember this day well, for duty took me to a remote island, sunbathed in fine weather, but drenched with sea spray during wild storms, and I thought that never at any season had I seen it so altogether quiet and peaceful. As I crossed the sound the wild, spirit-like call of a greenshank on migration awaked the echoes, and on my way I passed buzzards and ravens sailing contentedly in the sunshine. But that afternoon a ring of rainbow colours was formed round the sun, and it is rarely indeed that this is seen unless it be to herald a coming storm or a spell of unsettled weather.

The weather broke on the third of the month, and strong winds, with rain, were experienced almost daily till the 15th, when a spell of more settled weather set in. During the first period the wildest night was that of 11th-12th, when a torrential rainfall, with thunder and lightning, and accompanied by a gale from the west, visited the whole of the western Highlands. A rainfall of 4½ inches was measured at Fort William during a period of little over twelve hours, while at Achnasheen, in Ross-shire, over 4.60 inches of rain fell during the same period. On the 12th I saw numbers of Arctic skuas, both adult and immature birds, sheltering from the storm in a quiet arm of the sea where I had never before seen them. They had apparently been on their southward migration, and had been blown too far in to the east, for I should think that their usual line of flight must be considerably to the westward of where I saw them. There were many gulls and a few kittiwakes fishing here, and the skuas were, in their usual freebooting manner, pursuing any gull that had captured a fish, till he was forced to disgorge.

Fishing in company with a number of gulls, it was a pleasant surprise to see a tern. I have never before seen one in Scotland so late in the season. Evidently this wanderer was a migrant from the north and blown out of his course by the weather.

This storm was succeeded by one day of fair, though showery weather, during the evening of which the glass commenced to fall rapidly, and this fall was continued the following morning, when very heavy rain fell, though unaccompanied by wind. Without warning, shortly after midday, a whole gale sprang up from the south-west, approaching hurricane force about 1 p.m., when the barometer stood at 28.7 inches. Every burn was overflowing its banks, several railways were blocked by bridges being washed away, or by landslides, and important roads were rendered impassable for weeks. On the 15th, with a wind which had shifted to north-west, the hills were snow-covered, and a considerable quantity had fallen at an elevation of three thousand feet. On the 16th the snow line was lower, snow lying at the side of the road at an altitude of a thousand feet above sea level, and stags were driven down to their winter quarters, where many fine beasts were shot—a good ending to an indifferent season. As the heather this year was later than usual in coming into bloom, the unusual sight was witnessed in October of heather plants in full blossom, with snow covering the ground near by.

Following the spell of wild weather, more settled conditions were experienced up to the end of the month, enabling the crops to be secured in fairly good order, but on the 30th the glass again fell, and strong winds and rain marked the closing days.

Of migration I saw little in October. During one or two dark nights I heard the calling of ringed plover, and from time to time, notably on the 22nd, flocks of red-wings and fieldfares were passing.

The closing week of the month was eventful in one West Highland loch by reason of the great shoals of herring which arrived from the open sea in their millions.

3.—NOVEMBER

As yet no really wintry weather has visited the western seaboard. Much of the month was remarkable for its mildness and the only continued cold spell was felt about the middle of the month. On the 17th a heavy gale of easterly wind swept the whole of the west coast, and in certain districts was the most severe for a number of years. The gale lifted the surface of the water from the sea lochs, hurrying the spray before it in clouds, so that, looking against the sun—for the sun shone brightly throughout the gale—there appeared a layer of haze lying on the top of the water.

Flocks of redwings and fieldfares kept coming in through the month, and numbers of blackbirds with them. A few corn buntings were also on migration, and I heard one in song on the 14th. The prevailing winds—south and south-west—were against bird migration, and the number of migrants observed was comparatively few.

On the 4th the barometer stood very low—28.5 inches— with a gale from the south. On that day I made an expedition over some wild hill country fringing the coast. Even at this date the stooks of oats in certain cases still stood out in the crofters' fields. Drenching rain squalls accompanied the gale, and although the wind was off-shore, a swell rolling in told of heavy weather out to sea. Haunting the shore, grey crows were eagerly searching for any edible morsel—and they are not particular—cast up by the tide, and little grebes were diving in the shallow water. The hill burns were in spate, and the noise of rushing

206

Autumn in the Western Highlands

waters mingled with the roar of the wind as it struck the rocks on the bare hill faces. On the highest tops a thin coating of snow lay, and made one think of the ptarmigan on the wind-swept plateau, already assuming their winter plumage of white.

Where a sea loch runs several miles inland a small company of birds, seven or eight in number, were conspicuous. They were immature specimens of the red-throated diver, probably from the sub-arctic latitudes, on their way south. As they moved and dived the white plumage of their under parts showed up clearly against the dark water. At the head of the loch I passed through a sheltered wood of Scots firs. Here no wind penetrated, and the bracken, long and luxuriant, was still untouched by the frost, its green fronds a pleasing feature to the eye on this grey November day. From here the road led rapidly upwards, and the gale met one with full strength. Birches fringed each small hill burn. Less than a week previously they were resplendent in hues of orange and russet, but the gale had stripped them of most of their leaves, and even as I passed, these were caught up in swirling clouds and hurried overhead. A few rowans mingled with the birches, their leaves a subdued red or flaming crimson, and there is no tree that shows more beautiful tints than the rowan or mountain ash. Reaching an elevation of over one thousand feet the road crossed a stretch of boggy moorland, devoid of a single tree, but showing abundant signs of an ancient forest in the jagged stumps protruding from the peat. Here the gale was so powerful that progress against it was difficult, and the only life to be seen was a covey of grouse which rose suddenly and flew down wind at express speed.

With the coming of darkness the moon showed herself at intervals from behind scurrying clouds, and the weather cleared somewhat. Deer—stags and hinds—had come down to the glen to feed and crossed the road before me, one stag in particular making an enormous bound in his excitement. On reaching my destination the moon was commencing to dip towards the horizon to the south, and I saw the unusual phenomenon of a perfect lunar rainbow, every colour ghostly but complete, spanning the northern sky.

There are probably few people other than bird lovers who have ever heard the song of the dipper or water ouzel; he is so exclusive in his singing, and chooses such an unlooked-for season for his song. Yet his voice is of the sweetest, and, indeed, is surpassed by few birds. The dipper usually sings standing on a stone in the middle of a rushing hill burn. Sometimes he sings on the wing also. His notes are unlike those of any other bird. I have sometimes thought that his song a little resembled that of the wren, but in it there is much more music and melody than in that of the wee bird I have mentioned. The song is commenced early in November, and there is a certain dipper of my acquaintance which has been singing regularly during the past month just where a hill burn empties itself into a sea loch. I do not know whether water ouzels can be reckoned as migratory in the true sense of the word, but there is no doubt that they leave the uplands at the commencement of winter, and remain at the estuaries of streams and rivers and also along the margins of sea lochs during the cold season. On such a loch one morning I saw more than half a dozen of these birds feeding close together, their companions being turnstones and redshanks.

With the close of each nesting season a common gull has for the past seven years taken up his quarters on the lawn of a certain house in the Island of Mull. Every season he leaves his winter friends towards the end of March when, I imagine, he returns to his nesting-grounds. He can readily be identified, for he has only one leg, yet he is surprisingly active despite this handicap. He is known by his benefactors as "Gully," and to this name he readily responds. Each morning the inmates of the house share their porridge with him, and when called he comes confidently to the doorstep to receive his ration.

One season he returned to his winter quarters as early as July, but it is generally August before he arrives. He may be considered a remarkably fortunate bird in having an assured and plentiful food supply throughout the months of winter.

CHAPTER XXXV

WINTER IN THE WESTERN HIGHLANDS

I.—DECEMBER

ALTHOUGH during the month that has just closed there were many wild and stormy days, December will be remembered for a spell of magnificent calm and frosty weather which opened on the 12th and continued till the evening of the 20th. During the whole of this period the weather was calm, and latterly a light fall of snow covered the ground. The glass was low—29.4 inches or thereabouts—and this seems to bear out the fact that in winter, at all events, the finest weather is accompanied by a low, or comparatively low, barometer. At midday on the 20th, a ring appeared encircling the sun, and a thick blanket of cloud overspread the sky from the south, bringing wind with it at sunset. Cold, unsettled weather continued till the 28th, and the hills were heavily covered with snow. On the 28th, with a gale from the south-west, the temperature exceeded 50° Fahr., remaining high till the close of the month. On the 30th a strong gale blew from south-west, veering to the west, after heavy squalls of hail and rain, this being, I think, the heaviest wind experienced throughout the month.

Purple sandpipers have frequented the shore during December. On the 16th I noticed three purple sandpipers and two turnstones feeding together. It was interesting to watch the different methods by which they gained their food. The sandpipers confined themselves in their search to the immediate water's edge, whereas the turnstones were not so particular. In feeding, the sandpiper's movements resembled those of dunlin or sanderling, the bill being thrust down into the seaweed with great rapidity, reminding one of the action of an hydraulic riveter. All the while they were feeding they kept up a twittering cry, pleasant to the ear. The turnstones fed at a considerable distance from the water, and were actively engaged in turning over stones in their search for food—thus fully justifying their name. They covered a greater range in their feeding than the sandpipers. The purple sandpiper is a northern nesting bird, and is found far into the Arctic Circle during the summer months. There is a belief that it may sometimes nest in this country, though its eggs have not so far been found. Young birds scarcely able to fly may have been seen on the Farne Islands.

Black-headed gulls were with us in large numbers. On the 17th I saw an individual which had already assumed the black head of the nesting season—a very early date. About this time I watched a young herring gull of the year which was showing considerable ingenuity in its feeding. Standing on a flat-topped rock, just awash, it was endeavouring to catch numbers of the wily limpet. Limpets begin to feed directly they feel the water over them, and as each wavelet broke over the rock the gull made quick rushes to grab the limpets as they moved, and before they had time to re-fasten themselves to the rock. I could not see what success the bird was having, but admired its ingenuity.

At the end of the month red-throated divers were numerous. I saw one emerge with a crab in its bill. A herring gull swooped down. Like a flash the diver submerged, but in the excitement of the moment must have lost his hold of the crab, for the gull pounced triumphantly and carried it to a boat, where it proceeded to peck it at its leisure. In the meantime the diver dived once more, and was not long in reappearing with another crab of about the same size. Profiting by its unpleasant experience, the diver made desperate efforts to swallow the crab whole, and at length, by the help of copious draughts of water, succeeded in doing this, even while the gull was having great trouble with its stolen crab, and had by no means managed to dispose of it.

A shag was diving near, and it was interesting to compare its methods with those of the red-throated diver. When diving, the shag, and the cormorant also, throws itself out of the water with neck outstretched. It is this that causes the splash. The diver, on the other hand, stretches out his neck as he dives, but does not raise himself in the water. The result is that the dive is noiseless and scarcely a ripple is made to disturb the surface. When swimming the diver is normally higher in the water than either the shag or cormorant, and the neck is not so outstretched, so that in appearance it rather resembles a large duck. The red-throated species is the smallest as well as the most numerous of British divers, and is plentiful during winter on most parts of the coast.

2.—JANUARY

THE month of January was uniformly cold, with an almost entire absence of south-westerly gales of wind. Breezes from some easterly point were prevalent, and on the 12th and 13th there was a whole gale from the north north-east, with a high sea. Much frost was experienced towards the end of the month, and snow lay deep on the higher grounds. Many birds frequented the sheltered bays and sandy beaches of the shore line.

Long-tailed duck were numerous. Even on the first of the month some of them were going in pairs, but it is a common occurrence for birds of all species to be led into mating prematurely following upon a spell of mild weather in mid-winter, such as was experienced during December.

On a still day early in the month I had a good view of several grey plover feeding quite near me. Their breasts and under parts were pure white, so that when facing me they seemed almost as white as seagulls. As is the case with several waders, they have a strip of white feathers extending over and behind the eye, and seem to have some white on the forehead also. They resemble in size the golden plover, but are more handsome and conspicuous in their winter plumage. In their feeding the grey plover frequent the mud flats, often consorting with flocks of smaller waders, whereas the golden plover seem to prefer the green fields adjoining the sea.

Many herring gulls were busy breaking the shells of mussels by dropping them from a height, so that they might feed on their luckless owners. Several excursions into the air were often necessary before the shell was broken, and one gull that I watched dropped its mussel no fewer than a dozen times without result, and succeeded in breaking it only at the thirteenth effort.

On the 16th, a clear, frosty day, with two inches of snow on the ground, I watched a pair of red-breasted mergansers courting. With much bowing and outstretching of the neck the drake circled round the duck, both birds swimming very near together. On the 24th a large flock of godwit and knot performed wonderful evolutions in the strong wind before alighting to feed. A number of great northern divers are meanwhile distributed along the coast. I think I am right in saying that this diver remains under water longer and moves farther during submersion than any other bird. A dive of ninety seconds' duration is not unusual, and during this time the bird is all the while moving rapidly beneath the water.

3.—FEBRUARY

THE month was not many days old when a severe storm of wind and snow swept from the north-east across the Western Highlands. At the entrance to the lonely sea loch a heavy sea was running, so that the spray broke in clouds over the little rocky island where the storm petrel has her home in summer. All day and through the night the wind raged, but at daybreak the sky cleared and the wildness of the storm had passed. Towards afternoon I made my way to a rocky headland, holding concealed a small clachan, and also a beautiful sandy beach. Many curlew were feeding there. Every now and again one heard their clear whistling, and once or twice an individual would utter that trilling cry which is associated in the mind with days of spring and early summer. A heavy sea was still running, and on the beach masses of tangle weed were lying. Leaving the beach and proceeding towards the headland, one comes to a point where, high above great rocks and jutting reefs, one can watch the seas roll in with thunder.

One notices and is impressed by the great contrast between the waters of the Atlantic and those of the North Sea during these winter months. The Atlantic is green or blue, perhaps, even after a heavy gale, while the North Sea is repellent and muddy under similar conditions. Out to sea, perhaps a hundred yards from the shore, a small flock of long-tailed ducks were riding on the heaving waters. They caught the sunlight, the drakes especially, with their handsome black and white plumage. They were feeding at the sea bottom, and at short intervals dived down one after the other.

One could see through the glass that the drakes and ducks were calling to each other, but the rush of the waves drowned their cries. Near them were guillemots, and a solitary scoter drake—jet black against the waters—made its way out to sea.

At the headland there arises a sharp and steep hill sheer from the surface of the sea. Here one catches the full force of the wind, and a wide view meets the eye. No craft of any kind was in sight on this day, but a great stretch of waters, desolate and reflecting the cold light from the clear sky above them. Perhaps twenty miles to the northward one could see plainly the white towers of the lighthouse on Rudha Stoer. Even the spray from the Atlantic rollers could be made out, through the glass, breaking high in the air over the dark rocks. The sun sets early these February days, and soon he sank behind the hills to the south-west, and the waters took on a steel-blue colour. North-westward one saw the un-dulating outline of one of the Outer Hebrides, the higher ground snowbound. And so the winter night descended apace. The wind, too, died down, and with the darkness the frost descended on the western coast and bound the land in its firm grip.

On the 11th of the month I watched a large flock of green plover apparently migrating north. The wind was against them, and they were flying high and making slow progress. On the 24th I visited a nesting site of the raven. The day was a grand one, clear and sunny, with the sea as calm as a hill loch on a breezeless day. A three-mile row brought me to a narrow rock-girt gully running down from the heather-clad hillside above, to where the surf grinds the smooth, rounded pebbles at its entrance. The gully is full open to the south, and when a south-westerly gale blows, great rollers thunder in, so that at times the spray is borne even to the sheltered ledge on which the raven has her nest. One of the Gaelic-speaking fishermen who rowed me informed me that on the previous day he had seen four ravens leave the rock, but it was not until I had landed and stood almost beneath the nest that the owner flew out. Apparently she was already sitting, but I was not able to see into the nest, as this was built in a position inaccessible except with the aid of a rope. For a time the raven flew round restlessly, then disappeared; but a few minutes later at least three birds flew quickly past. It is unusual for several of these birds to be seen together during the spring of the year, and it may be that on this occasion the two parent birds were engaged in expelling, or attempt-ing to expel, one of their offspring of the previous season.

These rough notes may be of interest as showing the remarkable contrasts in weather and the variety of bird life to be met with during an average year in that Land of the Hills and the Glens adjoining the Atlantic.

INDEX

Index

Index

Index

Index

Index

Index

PRINTED BY
CASSELL & COMPANY, LIMITED,
LA BELLE SAUVAGE, LONDON, E.C.4

WS - #0171 - 071024 - C0 - 229/152/16 - PB - 9781332303533 - Gloss Lamination